More Cat Tales
of the
Old West

Triumphs, Trials & Trivia
of Frontier Felines

PRESTON LEWIS

San Angelo, Texas

ISBN: 978-1-964830-02-5
Imprint: Bariso Press

Edited by: Harriet Kocher Lewis
Cover design by: Jim Bean and Preston Lewis

Library of Congress Control Number: 2024910920

Cover Photo Courtesy of West Texas Collection,
Angelo State University
Printed in the United States of America

With Thanks and Appreciation
to
Western Writers of America

CONTENTS

Preston Lewis

FOREWORD

Sigmund Freud once said, "Time spent with cats is never wasted." That's exactly how I feel reading award-winning author Preston Lewis's book *More Cat Tales of the Old West: Triumphs, Trials & Trivia of Frontier Felines.* I've spent more than thirty years writing about women of the American Frontier and until recently, never thought much about cats in rough and tumble Western locations like Tombstone, Dodge City, or Leadville. No sooner had I read *Cat Tales of the Old West: Poems, Puns & Perspectives on Frontier Felines,* Lewis's first entertaining book on the subject, and learned about the proliferation of cats West of the Mississippi, did I happen onto my own tale of the furry mouse catchers set in Deadwood, South Dakota.

The story involves a grizzled, pale-eyed muleskinner named Phatty Thompson who, in 1876, drove his wagon down Deadwood's main thoroughfare toward one of the town's most popular dance halls. In the back of his vehicle was a load of frightened cats that were meowing and hissing. The distressed animals watched the sight of the budding mining community pass by them from their crude, wooden crates. The eyes of the scared felines were large and round; their ears were lying back on their heads, and most were huddled into a ball, terrified to be caged and unsure of what was happening.

Phatty proudly smiled at the townspeople who were craning their necks to get a better view of the cargo. When at last he arrived at his destination, several women of ill repute hurried out of the establishment where they worked and happily greeted the cat wrangler. The excited women wasted no time selecting the cat they wanted for their own, and, after paying Phatty between $10 to $40 for the precious pets, the soiled doves hurried off with their treasures. Loneliness was the businesswomen's motivation for their purchases.

Like Phatty's cargo, felines had a place in the history of the American West. In San Francisco and in other parts of the Gold Country, cats were in abundance. Articles about the care and feeding of cats occasionally appeared in Bay area newspapers and often criticized cat owners for neglecting their animals. A story in the August 28, 1872, edition of the *San Francisco Examiner* pointed out the numerous ways cat owners were unknowingly mistreating their pets.

"First. That a cat will not "hunt" so well if it has meat given to it. Now hunting is a cat's natural instinct, whether hungry or not. And even were it otherwise, the object of keeping a cat—driving away vermin—is affected by the sight and sound of a cat merely. Not to give cat meat is a cruel mistake because their stomachs, like those of all carnivorous animals, are adapted especially for the digestion of flesh and fish. To give a cat cake, bread, scraps, fat, or vegetables, which great hunger alone will induce it to touch, is apt to cause disorders of different forms. One frequent complaint, house cats' want of neatness, where they are kept much indoors, is owing to this mistaken diet.

"Now, to take up the neat class of cat owners (they ought to be taken up literally as well as on paper), those who think, or rather who do not think, but take for granted that cats can live on what they catch. Have any of these people reflected upon how many mice per week a cat can possibly find in a neighborhood of modern, well-built city houses, with cement-floors and plastered cellars, and concrete-paved wood and coal sheds, perhaps, and all the other excellent mice and vermin-proof appliances of modern times?!

"Our city if full of half-fed cats, whose owner's servant daily waste in the kitchen enough to keep them all well, if the lady of the house would only make it as much her daily duty to see that puss is fed after every meal, as she would see to her canary's seed-box and water glass, if she keeps one. If anyone in whose house there is a cat is too busy, too lazy, or too poor, to feed it properly, let the poor animal be dispatched with a sponge of chloroform.

"We should do better by these furry creatures. If readers observe the poor appearance of cats in homes where no one seems to care, they should request the animal be better fed in the future."

In 1874, Oakland, California, was known as the "great cat city in America." Cats were seen there at almost any time of the day and heard at any time of night. An article in the June 12, 1874, edition of the *Oakland Tribune* noted, "If Oakland honestly enjoys a reputation for one thing, it does it in the cat business." The article included an incident in connection with that claim.

"A showman who was exhibiting an anaconda in Sacramento, and giving it daily a rabbit for food, having occasion to print some 'poster' bills, telegraphed his agent in San Francisco to 'send two hundred cuts immediately.' The agent read the word cuts as cats, and thinking the manager proposed to change the diet of the snake, sent out an army of men catching cats, and by night was able to ship nearly a hundred. The agent, in apologizing for not sending the whole two hundred, said he hoped the snake would have enough to 'stay his stomach' until he could go over to Oakland, as Oakland was full of cats, and he thought he could fill the order at one haul."

As a writer of history, I find *More Cat Tales of the Old West: Triumphs, Trials & Trivia of Frontier Felines* is a helpful research tool. As a reader fascinated by the stories of such creatures, it's pure entertainment.

Chris Enss, *New York Times* Bestselling Author

Chapter One

Cats, Me and Twain

U nlike other animals of the Old West, cats traipse lightly across the ensuing pages of frontier history. There's the thunder of stampeding longhorns or the rumble of buffalo on the move. Or, wolves howling at the moon and coyotes yelping at anything. Then there's their canine cousins the dogs that make regular appearances on the streets or in the meadows working sheep, another source of friction on the frontier. Then there's the beasts of burden such as horses, oxen, mules and donkeys that carried or pulled pioneers and their provisions toward their dreams. Even birds make regular appearances in Old West histories like the canaries in mineshafts, hawks and eagles in the sky or buzzards on the ground consuming carrion.

And while the screech of cougars and bobcats sometimes makes it into the history books, the meows of the kitty cats, both domesticated and feral, have largely been ignored in 21st century accounts of frontier life. That was a fact I uncovered in 2016 when a journal editor asked me to develop a story on cats in the Old West. While my research library turned up less than a dozen references to cats, I had much better success on *newspapers.com*, culling period news articles about cats. In addition to that original article, my subsequent research on the frontier's mysterious, mischievous and noisy cats ultimately resulted in feline stories in both *Wild West* and *Journal of the Wild West History Association* as well as *Cat Tales of the Old West: Poems, Puns & Perspectives on Frontier Felines*, the predecessor to this volume.

More Cat Tales of the Old West: Triumphs, Trials & Trivia of Frontier Felines continues the unsung story of cats on the frontier through the newspaper accounts of the time as they originally appeared in the 19th century. Consequently, you'll find inconsistencies in spellings of some words like tom cat versus tomcat. I've tried to stay as close as possible to the original printed versions of the articles I have reproduced, though I do occasionally correct spelling or add punctuation for clarity.

Though I'm not a cat person, tending to favor canines over felines, I enjoy history, especially lesser known aspects of frontier life. Cats certainly fall into the obscure category when viewing frontier daily life from more than a century's distance. While cats may be subdued in Old West history books, they were far from silent during their time, their noisy nighttime concerts and confrontations a common complaint against the animals in spite of all the good they did in controlling rodents. Cats were truly the Jekyll and

Hyde of frontier mammals, a trait that caught my interest and led me to extensive research into the subject.

With a background in journalism, I have written dozens of articles throughout my writing career, but the bulk of my published work has been as a novelist, publishing more than forty western and historical novels. Quite by accident, I included cats in my novel *Mix-Up at the O.K. Corral*, an offbeat look at the famous Tombstone gunfight, which Bantam published in 1996. While doing research for the comic western, I read that Tombstone was overrun with rats and mice so I thought it would be fun to have my protagonist rustle cats elsewhere and sell them for an exorbitant profit whenever he returned to Tombstone. What I thought was a clever idea at the time I was writing my novel turned out to have been a frontier reality in the mining West. My subsequent research showed that such "cat drives" were common in mining country. A gold or silver rush always spawned a cat rush by clever entrepreneurs all intent upon making profit from selling cats to control rodents.

In my fictional Tombstone account, I had a cat that was so mean my protagonist H.H. Lomax could not sell him and kept him in his house instead. I named the cat "Satan," as that seemed to fit his personality because he regularly attacked or ambushed Lomax whenever he was in town. As I wrote my novel, one thing led to another and Satan went on to become a pivotal character in resolving the plot. However, Satan, bless his feline heart, led me to my first encounter with cat fanatics as editors. Believe me, you don't want to mess with this type of editor.

Their names were Elizabeth Tinsley and Pam Lappies, both delightful and talented editors who worked for Book Creations Inc., which was editing my series for Bantam.

During the editing process they notified me that they had a serious problem with my cat, Satan. I was stumped and concerned at what it could possibly be because I had treated the tomcat better in the manuscript than he had treated my protagonist, even if Lomax was away for weeks on end from the house he shared with the malicious tomcat. Now get this, Pam and Liz were distraught that Satan, a despicable creature to begin with, could not get out of the house to find food and water for sustenance in Lomax's absence.

Think about that, will you? Now consider this, I'm dealing with a fictional cat that doesn't exist except on the pages of my novel. My editors, though, were concerned that my imaginary cat couldn't get out of a nonexistent house, to find food that isn't there so he doesn't starve to death, even though he's never lived to begin with, except in my mind and on the pages of my manuscript. I argued it was ridiculous, but they insisted otherwise and convinced me to include a sentence in the novel that indicated a hole in the floor allowed Satan to squeeze through whenever he needed to get out for sustenance. I suppose on the positive side of my editors' concerns, they at least didn't badger me into forcing my protagonist to empty the litter box after each trip back to Tombstone. Subsequently, I learned that Liz and Pam were not only cat lovers but also had a couple felines roaming the BCI offices for companionship.

Twenty years later, I reconnected with the two editors to let them know that *The Memoirs of H.H. Lomax* series I had started with them would be returning to print and I would be doing more books in the series—five to date—though none with cats as characters. Liz responded, "That's terrific news about Lomax, whom I occasionally mention or even quote to this day. He's more real to me than Billy the Kid or Doc Holliday or the James boys. My favorite guy. And, of course, Pam and I adored working with you and all the rest of the crazy characters you brought into our humdrum BCI lives (the cat Satan comes to mind)." I reckon Liz and Pam had been right after all, as providing a way for Satan to find sustenance in Lomax's absence had kept him alive in the minds of my editors for more than two decades.

In *More Cat Tales of the Old West: Triumphs, Trials & Trivia of Frontier Felines* I return to the news clippings of old to bring some new perspectives on cats in the history of the American West. I follow this introduction with the chapter *Odds and Ends and Cats*, a potpourri of the feline accounts that struck the fancies of Old West editors. Next comes *Domesti*cat*ed*, which examines cats on the home front, including their defense of family and their unusual "jobs." In *Cats versus Rats (and Others)* I explore the eternal battle between felines and rodents with a few other animals thrown in. *Cat Burglaries and Other Crimes* looks at the dark side of frontier cats that got away with murder, felonies and misdemeanors. The chapter on *Cattle Drives* chronicles the entrepreneurs who profited immensely by rushing cats to mining strikes to combat the overwhelming rodent problem. Once the pussycats reached the mining districts, they

created news as is demonstrated in *Cat Prospecting.*
Then in the chapter *Curtain and Cat Calls,* I examine
cats as entertainers, sometimes intentionally and
sometimes not.

In selecting news clips for inclusion, I looked for
interesting or unusual stories that illustrated human
interactions with or observations of cats. Sometimes
the accounts are amusing, sometimes cringe-worthy,
but readers should remember attitudes, particularly in
the frontier West, were largely different then than
they are today toward cats and other animals as
valued companions. Save for their rodent control,
cats were often more nuisance than companion. In
doing my research, I focused on newspapers west of
the Mississippi River and selected stories published in
those papers between 1860 and 1900. Most of the
articles relate to cats from the West, but some were
reprinted from eastern newspapers. I have included
some of these because they illustrate the public's—or
at least the editor's—fascination with cats. My
database search turned up 7.14 million hits for cats.
By comparison, a database search for dogs during that
same period came up with 4.48 million possibilities.
Cats, for all their annoyances, still seemed to captivate
the public more than their canine counterparts.

Nineteenth century American newspapers often
swapped editions with other papers regionally and
even nationally, granting each other permission to
reprint stories in their own journals. This practice or
"Exchange," as it was known, allowed papers to share
news accounts, meaning that a cat story that first
appeared in Texas might show up in Utah, muddying
the actual location of the original incident. Often
these clippings were marked as "Exchange" or "Ex."

to designate their source. Some of the selected excerpts pulled from the newspaper columns had headings, while others did not. For readability and graphic consistency, I have added headings to ease the transition between clippings. Headings I supplied have been *italicized* to differentiate them from original headings as they appeared in newspapers of the time.

Nearly all of what follows came from anonymous journalists and readers, whose names have been lost to history. However, to end this introduction, I chose to reprint a Mark Twain account of one young man's fall for cats. Before he became a world-famous novelist, Twain traveled the West and reported on it as a journalist in Virginia City, Nevada, before his wit and skill with the written word earned him space in some of the nation's largest newspapers as well as the book contracts that made him famous.

In his later years, Twain was a great lover of cats, even being reported at one point in his life as having nineteen cats of his own. When he traveled on some of his later speaking engagements, he could not take his pets with him so in many locations he actually rented cats to provide company when he was away from home and family. With his brood cats, Twain assigned them all names, such as Bambino, Beelzebub, Blatherskite, Buffalo Bill, Sin, Soapy Sal, Sour Mash, Pestilence and my favorite, Satan. Yes, the great American novelist Mark Twain had a real cat named Satan before I created my imaginary one.

Though no cat is named in Twain's Jim Wolf and the Tom-Cats, the story reflects Twain's sense of humor and his observational skills. Written in dialect, the story originally appeared in the Sunday *New York Mercury* on July 14, 1867.

Jim Wolf and the Tom-Cats

I knew by the sympathetic glow upon his bald head—I knew by the thoughtful look upon his face—I knew by the emotional flush upon the strawberry on the end of the old liver's nose, that Simon Wheeler's memory was busy with the olden time. And so I prepared to leave, because all these were symptoms of a reminiscence—signs that he was going to be delivered of another of his tiresome personal experiences—but I was too slow; he got the start of me. As nearly as I can recollect, the infliction was couched in the following language:

"We was all boys, then, and didn't care for nothing, and didn't have no troubles, and didn't worry about nothing only how to shirk school and keep up a revivin' state of devilment all the time. Thish-yar Jim Wolf I was a talking about, was the 'prentice, and he was the best-hearted feller, he was, and the most forgivin' and onselfish I ever see—well, there couldn't a more bullier boy than what he was, take him how you would; and sorry enough I was when I see him for the last time.

"Me and Henry was always pestering him and plastering hoss-bills on his back and putting bumble-bees in his bed, and so on, and sometimes we'd crowd in and bunk with him, not'thstanding his growling, and then we'd let on to get mad and fight acrost him, so as to keep him stirred up like. He was nineteen, he was, and long, and lank, and bashful, and we was fifteen and sixteen, and tolerable lazy and worthless.

"So, that night, you know, that my sister Mary give the candy-pullin', they started us off to bed early, so as the comp'ny could have full swing, and we rung in on Jim to have some fun.

"Our winder looked out onto the roof of the ell, and about ten o'clock a couple of old tom-cats got to rairin' and chargin' around on it and carryin' on like sin. There was four inches of snow on the roof, and it was froze so that there was a right smart crust of ice on it, and the moon was shining bright, and we could see them cats like daylight. First, they'd stand off and e-yow-yow-yow, just the same as if they was a cussin' one another, you know, and bow up their backs and bush up their tails, and swell around and spit, and then all of a sudden the gray cat he'd snatch a handful of fur out of the yaller cat's ham, and spin him eround, like the button on a barn-door. But the yaller cat was game, and he'd come and clinch, and the way they'd gouge, and bite, and howl; and the way they'd make the fur fly was powerful.

"Well, Jim, he got disgusted with the row, and 'lowed he'd climb out there and shake him off'n that roof. He hadn't reely no notion of doin' it, likely, but we everlastin'ly dogged him and bullyragged him, and 'lowed he'd always bragged how he wouldn't take a dare, and so on, til bimeby he highsted up the winder, and lo and behold you, he went—went exactly as he was—nothin' on but a shirt, and it was short. But you ought to a seen him! You ought to seen him cre-e-epin' over that ice, and diggin' his toenails and his fingernails in for to keep from slippin'; and 'bove all, you ought to seen that shirt a flappin' in the wind, and them long, ridicklous shanks of his'n a-glistenin' in the moonlight.

"Them comp'ny folks was down there under the eaves, the whole squad of 'em under that ornery shed of old dead Washn'ton Bower vines—all sett'n round about two dozen sassers of hot candy, which they'd sot in the snow to cool. And they was laughin' and talkin' lively; but bless you, they didn't know nothin' 'bout the panorama that was goin' on over their heads. Well, Jim, he went a-sneakin' and a-sneakin' up, onbeknowns to them tom-cats—they was a swishin' their tails and yow-yowin' and threatenin' to clinch, you know, and not payin' any attention—he went a sneakin' and a sneakin' right up to the comb of the roof, til he was, in a foot 'n' a half of 'em, and then all of a sudden he made a grab for the yaller cat! But by Gosh he missed fire and slipped his holt, and his heels flew up and he flopped on his back and shot off'n that roof like a dart!—went a smashin' and a-crashin' down through them old rusty vines and landed right in the dead center of all them comp'ny-people!—sot down like a yearth-quake in them two dozen sassers of red-hot candy, and let off a howl that was hark f'm the tomb! Them girls—well they left, you know. They see he warn't dressed for comp'ny, and so they left. All done in a second, it was just one little war whoop and a whish of their dresses, and blame the wench of was in sight anywhers!

"Jim, he was a sight. He was gormed with that bilin' hot molasses candy clean down to his heels, and had more busted sassers hanging' to him than if he was a Injun princess - and he came a prancin' up-stairs just a whoopin' and a cussin', and every jump he give he shed some china, and every squirm he fetched he dripped some candy!

"And blistered! Why bless your soul, that pore cretur couldn't reely set down comfortable for as much as four weeks."

Chapter Two

Odds and Ends and Cats

Almost from the beginning of recorded times, cats provided an endless source of human fascination. According to Jewish legend, Adam and presumably Eve kept a cat in the house to rid the place of mice. Ancient Egyptians worshipped cats so much that they forbade their killing. Historical evidence shows Greeks having cats in the fifth century B.C. and naming them "*ailouros*," meaning the animal with the waving tail. Early Romans initially kept weasels for rodent control but eventually replaced them with cats because of their better temperament and their superior skill in hunting rodents.

By the Middle Ages, various superstitions evolved about cats. Because of their mysterious ways, they came during those times to be associated with witchcraft and even Satan. As the Age of Discovery dawned, domestic cats spread from Europe to the rest of the world, accompanying exploration vessels for rodent control and good luck. Eventually, New World settlers brought cats to North America, where they ultimately thrived and eventually headed west with the pioneers.

As cats proliferated across North America, they became a source of continuing fascination because of their mysterious and aloof nature. Frontier newspapers regularly ran shorts and even full stories on the machinations of cats, whether locally or back east or even across the pond. Some western newspapers—or their editors at least—seemed especially fascinated with cats such as *The Record-Union* of Sacramento, California; *The Broad Ax* of Salt Lake City, Utah; *The Galveston Daily News* in Texas; and several newspapers in the Pacific Northwest.

Those newspapers were especially helpful in compiling this collection and its predecessor. Within this chapter will be found stories of a barking cat and several felines that disprove the old adage "you can't go home again." The chapter includes references to cats that saved lives, that survived the elements or their unfortunate circumstances, and that outwitted humans, their master or otherwise.

Just as life was hard on the men and women who inhabited the West, it presented challenges to cats as well. Like their pioneer companions, cats often made do with their wits and a bit of luck thrown in.

Cat Tales

A Philadelphia cat wears false teeth.

A Macon, Missouri, cat reared six young squirrels.

A litter of foxes is cared for by a Reading, Pennsylvania, tabby.

A cat known to be over 25 years old died at Tyro, Kansas, the other day.

Thirteen Brooklyn cats quarreled and fought until all but one were dead.

A Philadelphia man owns a cat that he claims has killed 2,500 mice during its lifetime.

In a mine near Butte, Montana, live hundreds of cats that have never seen the light of day.

Twenty years ago a cat race was held at Lancaster, Kentucky, in which there were 305 entries.

Margaret King, a New York woman, while intoxicated, cut a kitten into pieces with a pair of shears.

Sebastian, a big black cat owned by a Cumberland, Maryland, woman wears a diamond earring in each ear.

A cat in a Strand tavern in London has become intemperate through drinking wine spilled by waiters.

The Broad Ax, Salt Lake City, Utah
Saturday, November 4, 1899, p4

A Barking Cat
Nursed by a Foster Mother,
He Has Traits of the Dog

James H. Maddox, superintendent of the Missouri District Telegraph Company, has a cat. Besides the usual feline complement of nine lives, this cat has a past, and, unless all signs fail, a future which falls to the lot of few cats, says the *St. Louis Republic*.

His name is Towser, and, although his mother was a well-bred lady, Towser has all the characteristics, habits and frailties of a dog. In early kitten-hood Towser's mother fell a victim to the deadly cat rifle of a small boy, and Mr. Maddox found a foster mother for the kitten in a kind-hearted pet dog, with a young family and troubles of her own. The canine mother took kindly to the little foundling and Towser, the kitten, grew fat and sassy with a litter of puppy foster brothers and sisters.

When the kitten was weaned, he showed no tendency to abandon the dog's life which he had learned to lead and began to exhibit all the canine characteristics which he had nursed with his adopted mother's milk. Instead of mewing and caterwauling like a melancholy orphan cat, he began to bark like the other puppies, and growl like they did, and he became the wonder of the friends and visitors at the Maddox home. He was named "Towser" and responds to the whistle of his master like a sure enough dog. Perhaps the oddest trick Towser has learned is that of wagging his tail, which he does, not in the serpentine manner of his ancestors, but from side to side, in the vigorous and uncompromising style of a dog. Towser expresses fear, too, as he has seen his foster brethren do, and runs to cover. During the hot weather Towser suffered considerably from the heat and might have been seen sitting about in the shade, panting with his tongue out, in the manner supposed to be peculiar to the dog.

He has none of the sinister traits of his tribe, does not parade along the narrow edge of back fences in the dead of night, and gets from place to place in a dog trot or a real gallop instead of in the soft-footed and obsequious manner of other cats. Towser has mastered that mysterious free-masonry of dogs which has been the wonder of naturalists for all time, and seems to have but little trouble in forming the acquaintance of strange dogs which he meets on the street corners and about the bases of friendly lamp posts and telegraph poles. Occasionally he has run across an ugly terrier, which, accepting no overtures, would attempt to rend Towser on the spot, and it is only on such rare occasions that Towser's feline propensities come to the surface. When a dog attacks him, he will climb a tree or a fence, where he will sit growling and barking at the enemy until he satisfies him that he is not really a cat, but a dog in all but physical conformation.

Towser is very fond of a run through the streets with his master, and from long jaunts over the granitoid pavements and rough streets his once velvet paws have been covered with callous corns until his footfall is no longer inaudible, and his toe-nails are as rough and strong as those of a dog.

Towser has a pronounced antipathy for women, and will rush at them, barking furiously and growling as if he would bite them; his bark is worse than his bite, however, for he has never been known to bite anyone and has earned for himself the reputation of being a very docile and intelligent dog, or cat, as the case may be.

The Broad Ax, Salt Lake City, Utah
Saturday, December 4, 1897, p3

A Cat Story

Last week when George Rordan moved his family from near the old mill site below the Parker mill, he brought in a box (with) the family cat, and five kittens, the latter just large enough to be playful, to his home. Of course, they came down by way of the wagon road, a distance of about six miles. The kittens had been born near the flume, and as Mr. Rordan lived near it, the mother cat at least seemed to understand it. After remaining in their new quarters two days, the old cat struck out for the mill, taking two of her kittens with her, and instead of taking the longer way by the wagon road, she "went up the flume," straight to her old quarters. The next night she came back and started with the other three kittens but lost one of them on the way, which being found served to disclose the route she had traveled. Now as the old cat had never been along the flume, and as she was taken from the old quarters in a closed box, how did she know that following up the flume would take her to her old home?

The Hood River (Oregon) *Glacier*
Saturday, September 10, 1892, p2

Cat Can Kansas

A cat that had been taken from Kansas to Indiana made its way back to Kansas, consuming about two months in the journey.

    The Advocate, Lakin, Kansas
    Thursday, May 20, 1897, p3

Heroic Sailor

During a heavy storm that prevailed in Port Townsend harbor last Saturday night, the steamer *Wildwood*, which made the run for the Thompson Friday and Saturday, sank while lying at her dock. A large hole was made in her hull by a drifting log. A man who was asleep on board was saved from drowning by the ship's cat, which awakened him by scratching his face just as the steamer was going down.

    The San Juan Islander, Friday Harbor, Washington
    Thursday, December 1, 1898, p3

The Cat that Came Along
**Got In a Trunk at Denver and
Came All the Way to Kansas City**

Everybody has heard about Puss in Boots and the Cat that Came Back and the Cat and the Cherub and the Cat that Killed the Rat that Ate the Malt that Lay in the House that Jack Built and various other catastrophes in the category of feline adventures and everybody thought the list was complete, but it isn't. It remained for a Denver cat to finish it. And this is the tale of the Cat that Came Along.

Last week a woman whose home is in Denver came to Kansas City to visit a family that lives on the East Side. She brought her little daughter and her trunk with her, and she brought something else, too, but she didn't know it until later in the day. She left Denver one afternoon and reached here the next morning. Her trunk didn't get out to the house where she was visiting until three hours after she did. Then it was carried up to her room, and, as is customary, the women on the family gathered there to chat and admire the "visiting clothes and hats."

In the course of an hour the tray was unpacked. The woman leaned over and lifted it out. As she did so, a piercing scream rent the air, and the two other women in the room did a high jump and landed in the middle of the bed, for out of the bottom part of the trunk had jumped a big cat.

But the cat wasn't a bit frightened. It walked slowly across the room and spread itself in a patch of sunlight without so much as a "meow."

"Where in the world did you come from?" exclaimed the Denver woman as she recognized her house cat. There was no answer. The cat was asleep. Its long journey in the bottom of a trunk, where it reposed on all sorts of spring gowns and jackets, is still unexplained. There are many theories as to how the cat chanced to get into the trunk. One thing only is certain. And that is that the cat came along. It wasn't going to miss a chance to visit the greatest city in the west.—*Kansas City Star.*

Arizona Republic, Phoenix, Arizona

Monday, April 24, 1899, p4

Feline Boomerang

B.F. Childs tells us that some time ago a tramp tomcat came to his house and has been feasting on birds in his yard ever since. Tuesday night he caught Mr. Thomas Cat, put him in a sack and then carried him two miles away and dropped him in the weeds. B.F. returned home and rested in peace that night. Yesterday morning he arose from his couch and going out into the yard he saw his tramp cat sitting on the doorstep [waiting]for the occupants of the house to throw open their hospitable doors.

Arkansas City (Kansas) *Daily Traveler*
Thursday, August 9, 1888, p3

Snake Harmer

Here is something to write "remorse" on the soul of the St. Louis editor indulged in a column of denunciation against cats last week. The *Sherman Register* tells the story, which is, doubtless, literally true: "A little three-year-old son of Mr. Tom Ed Bomar went out of the house into the yard and was followed by the house cat. Walking down a narrow pathway, hemmed on either side by a mass of rank weeds and grass, unconscious of danger and too young to know any fear, the child went, followed by his faithful playfellow.

Mr. Bomar was standing in the door watching his child, when he saw the cat suddenly spring upon something in the path about three feet in front of the child, and walking down the path to investigate the matter was horrified to see the cat battling with a large rattlesnake that had coiled itself in the pathway as if waiting for a victim, while the little child stood over them clapping his hands as if much amused and delighted. Mr. Bomar killed the snake, while the cat, although bitten in several places, is as good as a new one.

The Galveston (Texas) *Daily News*
Tuesday, August 24, 1875, p2

Pets Worth Having

A cat in Mississippi recently gave up its life to save the community. The river was very high, and the dike which had been built to keep out the waters gave way in one place and the water was pouring in unnoticed, when the cat passed by and, realizing the condition of affairs, crawled into the hole and stopped the flood. It is estimated that $80,000 and a number of lives were saved by the heroic feline, and the villagers have built a beautiful tomb of red granite, with mice carved in relief, over the bones of the animal.

Arkansas City (Kansas) *Daily Traveler*
Sunday, July 28, 1889, p8

Fell Into a Well.
A Smart Youth and a Cat
Have an Unpleasant Ducking

A Mexican boy named Juan Encinas was badly injured Wednesday by falling into a well. He with a couple of other boys were amusing themselves by throwing stones into the well. Encinas thought it would be a good joke to throw a cat into the water and he no sooner conceived the idea than he went into the house and returned with tabby. He leaned over the well holding the cat by the tail and was on the point of dropping the feline when he lost his balance and followed the cat. There was only about three feet of water, which was enough to break the force of the drop, but he had a leg broken and the cat made matters unpleasant by jumping on his head to keep out of the water and badly scratching him. His companions, frightened by what occurred, ran hastily away and informed nobody of the accident. The boy and the cat remained in the well fully an hour before being discovered. A rope was lowered and he was hauled to the surface along with his four-legged companion in misery.

The boy's face was a sight—deep furrows showing how kitty took revenge for the impromptu bath. The lad's leg is in a condition to keep him out of mischief for several weeks.

Arizona Republic, Phoenix, Arizona
Friday, August 21, 1896, p1

A Famished Cat's Prudence

At Osage City Mrs. C.A. Stoddard was cleaning up her garret when by some means the family cat got into an old trunk filled with clothing and was shut in tight and fast. Just twenty days later Mrs. Stoddard was in the garret again and heard the cat's feeble cry from the trunk. When the lid was lifted the cat had just strength enough to climb out. It had torn the clothing in the trunk all to pieces in its clawing, and had gnawed the sides nearly through in several places. But perhaps the most singular circumstance was found in the manner in which the cat took care of itself after securing its liberty. Mrs. Stoddard set before it a big dish of milk and a big dish of water. It would lap a little of each, and then lie down for a few minutes, when again it would partake sparingly of the milk and water, and this proceeding it continued through the whole afternoon. If that cat had been a human being, doubtless it would have swallowed all that was placed before it at one gulp.—*Kansas City Journal*

Statesman Journal, Salem, Oregon
Sunday, May 14, 1899, p4

Pussy's Long Fast

Lynn, Massachusetts, Special—On February 19 a live cat was dug out of a ruined building in this city. It is now known beyond a doubt that this animal had been confined in the ash-pit of an old-fashioned brick oven ever since the fire, November 26,1889. Instances of cats living from fifty to sixty days without food or drink have been known, but this one seems to have distanced all others. The old oven has not been used for over forty years, consequently nothing remained there for fodder. It may have been that mice and rats were confined with kitty and she made herself comfortable while they lasted. The place where the cat was confined is such that, when the smoking debris fell at the time of the fire, the hottest of ruins were only a few feet distant. The animal, when released, could only walk a few steps at a time without falling over on her side.

Morning Oregonian, Portland, Oregon
Wednesday, March 26, 1890, p6

A Sagacious Cat

There is a deep well on Mr. Joe Buchtel's place which has not been used for some time and has always been carefully covered except a small hole alongside the pump large enough for a cat to get through. Mr. H. Wastervelt, a neighbor, has a much-prized cat and several days ago the cat, chased by a dog, plunged into the hole and went down the well like a flash. How long it was in the well is not known, but Wednesday it managed to climb up the pump shaft to the top of the well to the opening. It was unable to get out, but made itself heard, and when an attempt was made to get the little creature out, it again fell back into the well. A bucket was then lowered; the cat got into the bucket and was quickly brought to the surface. It knew what the bucket was for. Who says a cat can't think?

Morning Oregonian, Portland, Oregon
Saturday, March 15, 1890, p11

The Cat Is a Fraud.

All the people who have ever had much to do with cats, say that they cannot be trusted. A dog will do as he has been taught, but a cat will only mind while it is watched. A lady who owns one has often whipped it for coming into the parlor, where, with its sharp claws, it tears up the curtains or anything else that flutters. While the lady is in the house the cat will never go into the parlor, but when she had been out she always finds pussy's black hairs on the parlor sofa cushions. The other day, when she came home from a call, she saw pussy in the parlor window lazily watching the people go by. When it saw her coming, it jumped and ran upstairs, where she found it pretending to be asleep.

The Seattle (Washington) *Star*
Monday, April 10, 1899, p2

The Black Cat Hoodoo

The mysterious black cat with the white forepaws, which brought woe upon the fire department, has had a fit, and the hoodoo is off. No longer do uncanny alarms come sounding at all hours of the night from uninhabited parts of the town. No more do the firemen find their horses suddenly lame, or the bolts dropping off their apparatus. All troubles of that sort have reached a happy end.

The cat crept into the station last Monday night, and before morning the department had responded to five alarms. Four of them were trivial affairs, but one was the hardest blaze that the fire boys had met in weeks. The crowning achievement of the cat was that night while No. 5 truck was making a run to the Plummer fire. The horses were galloping down Mallon Avenue at top speed, when as Monroe Street was reached, there was an ugly collision with car No.

13, which also was doing some sprinting. Both the car and the truck were mixed up for ten seconds, so it looked as if somebody must surely have been killed, but luckily, despite the black cat and the number of the car, nobody was hurt beyond being badly jarred.

And the next day the cat had a fit and since then the hoodoo has been off.—*Spokesman-Review*

The Seattle (Washington) *Star*
Wednesday, March 8, 1899, p3

Invincible Feline

An immortal cat has for a longtime annoyed Mr. B.F. Feeley, of Tremont, N.Y. It has been in his family for two years, and he has tried various ways to close its career. His last plan was by tying a brick to its back and dropping it in the Harlem. That same night it walked home, handicapped with the same brick.

The Yakima (Washington) *Herald*,
Thursday, March 10, 1898, p3

Up in a Balloon

Johnny Mish, living on Wall Street in this city, is in trouble today, in consequence of a distressing incident which proved fatal to his pet cat yesterday. Johnny's brother was the happy owner of half a dozen beef bladders, nicely dried and inflated, and stowed away in the house loft. Yesterday Johnny and his pet were playing together in the loft, and the little fellow attached the cord that held the bladders to the cat, as he sat by a window opening on to the kitchen roof.

Puss didn't enjoy the joke, and escaped through the window and ran up the roof, when a gust of wind bore her heavenward in the direction of the Cape. When last seen the curious balloon was moving in the direction of Alaska. Johnny would like to get puss back again, but he can't.

The Morning Astorian, Astoria, Oregon
Saturday, October 6, 1877, p1

Buzz Right Here

An Akron, Ohio, cat, relying upon his nine lives to save him, allowed his tail to swell, his spine to curve, and with the "banner cry of hell" emanating from his jaws, waded into a buzz saw that was in rapid motion. The cat was never seen again, but sawyer, who always stood with his mouth open while at work, remarked to his assistant that he could "taste" fiddle strings and sausage-meat in air that morning.—*Titusville Press*

The Galveston (Texas) *Daily News*
Thursday, December 12, 1872, p6

All Is Forgiven

Lord Locke had an adventure Tuesday night that he probably will not forget for some time. A poor little innocent cat took shelter beneath his sidewalk, and with sweet mew-sick tried to sing his lordship into the land of Morpheus. The serenade was not appreciated. He became angry and used hard names to the poor pussy. This would not do, so he began coaxing in his sweetest flow of eloquence. This the cat could not resist. He grabbed her with excited violence and threw her across the plaza. The cat's feelings were wounded and she returned to punish him with forgiveness and kindness. He again became excited, and with a big stone tried to send the cat to kingdom come. One of her lives departed for the golden shore, but eight remained to tantalize her would-be assassin. His lordship again became discouraged, but fascinated with her staying qualities. They now live happily together.

The Las Vegas (New Mexico) *Gazette*
Thursday, September 4, 1884, p4

Chapter Three

Domesticated

Home, job and recreation are the triad that make up the common adult's daily life. The same could be said for cats as they were covered in frontier newspapers.

Home encompassed family and shelter for humans. In the case of cats, domesticity likewise included both, shelter and family, though sometimes it was a blended family so to speak as cats on occasion adopted unusual members to their home and kinship. The feline brood didn't always limit familial bonds to their own kind. And sometimes, cats found unusual ways to provide food for themselves and their offspring.

The bonds of family are strong and sometimes parents must fend for their offspring's survival. Blessed with teeth and claws, mother felines on occasion had to fight to protect their kitties, sometimes at overwhelming odds. On those occasions, cats made news for sure.

As versatile and clever as cats were, they never had formal jobs per se. However, that doesn't mean they didn't work. Either through natural feline curiosity or entertainment, cats did find ways to help humans with their chores or needs. Thus, cats wound up with "jobs" or tasks as testers/tasters, as plumber's assistants, as fishers and as nut gatherers. One cat even liked to churn milk, earning him the eternal gratitude of his keeper.

Where "work" ends and recreation begins for cats is hard to say for often they are one and the same. So, what may have been work to the human, like churning milk, may well have been viewed and enjoyed by the cat as play.

Either way, cats certainly contributed to the success of the frontier household, if in no other way than in holding down damage and disease from rodents. When they went beyond that, either in their recreation, their defense of family or their "jobs," they and their accomplishments often appeared in frontier newspapers.

This Cat Works

Near Stockton, California, is a cat by the name of Bildad, whose mistress, Miss Angie Eddes, also owns some almond trees. When these nuts are ripe, and start to fall, Bildad begins work. His mistress sets a large basket out in the almond grove and goes back to the house. Then Bildad picks up all the plump brown nuts, and carries them to the basket, never stopping until it is full, when the useful cat goes in and pulls at the apron of its mistress to let her know that it should be emptied. Bildad can fill it again.

Bildad also churns. Mr. Eddes has made a treadle to work the churn, and upon this Bildad stands and churns away. The cat can tell by the sound of the milk when the butter has come, and strikes with his paw on the little bell to let his mistress know that he is through. Besides this Bildad plays and enjoys a romp as much as any other cat.

The Carlsbad (New Mexico) *Current*
Saturday, June 10, 1899, p3

A Singular Cat

Will Harte of Red Bluff has a peculiar cat; that is a cat with peculiar affections, her peculiarity being that she had adopted a grey squirrel as one of her family. She gave birth to a family of five kittens a short time ago, and three of them were killed. The squirrel was then put with the two remaining kittens, and it seems just as much at home as when out in the woods. It allows the kittens to scramble all over it and greets its adopted mother very effusively when she appears in the box where the family resides.

The foster mother suckles the squirrel as she does her kittens, and when the little fellow scampered out on the fence the other day she quickly followed, and catching the truant by the back of the neck, took him back into the box. The squirrel is about half grown, and is at perfect liberty to go and come at will, but it very seldom leaves the box.

Daily Capital Journal, Salem, Oregon
Tuesday, May 21, 1889, p3

Squirrel Whipped a Cat

There was a lively scrap at A.H. Trent's store yesterday, says the *Spokane Chronicle*, in which two men came near losing their fingers, while Patsy, the cat, was badly chewed up.

Trent is the possessor of a fine gray squirrel, and thought it would be a grand scheme to turn the squirrel out of the cage and give him the freedom of the store. The store doors were closed and the squirrel liberated.

For a few minutes the squirrel had a lively time chasing about, but came too near the cat. There was a maddened scream, and the air was full of fur and claws. An attempt was made to separate the combatants, in which Trent was bitten through the finger, and large chunks of cuticle were torn from his hands. His clerk came to his assistance and fared no better. The squirrel and cat continued to fight while the bleeding human referees stood and looked on.

At last, the cat got loose, escaped through the back window, and has not been seen since. The squirrel returned to his cage, proud of his victory, having cleaned up all in sight.

The Eugene (Oregon) *Guard*
Friday, April 24, 1896, p1

New Use for Cats
A Plumber Utilizes Them
In Locating Leak
In Drainage Piping

A new wrinkle in the plumbing business was brought to light this week which will evidently revolutionize the old order of things. The difficulty in locating leaks in water and drainage pipes is very great in New York houses, and in such large establishments as the Vanderbilts' and Astors' a man is hired by the year to examine the plumbing and keep it in good condition. But in spite of such rigid care, the house drains will occasionally get defective and defy the most expert plumber.

To meet the needs of the modern system of plumbing, a genius in this line of work has tacked up a sign to the effect that he makes a specialty of locating leaks in the drains. The success of this new enterprise was assured this week. The owner of a Fifth Avenue mansion having reason to suspect that the drains in his house were defective, plumber after plumber was called in to make examination. But all to no effect. The leak could not be found.

As a last resort he called in the new plumber, whose methods of procedure were so entirely different from those adopted by his other brother tradesmen. Instead of bringing a kit of tools and a plumber's assistant, he brought into the house a mysterious-looking basket. Then requesting the owner of the mansion to let him have free access to all of the rooms, he proceeded to business. A strong infusion of valerian was poured into the pipes. Three large, sleek-looking cats were then taken from the basket and the establishment thrown open to their inspection. The plan succeeded marvelously well. As is well known, a curious property of valerian is the attraction of its smell for cats. These animals seem to sniff the odor from a long distance, and will invariably follow the scent.

The three cats thus let loose soon discovered the two leaks, as each one or two of them took their position in order to enjoy the pungent odor at their leisure. The leaks being discovered, the work of repair was very simple. The plumber received a good round sum for his work and now enjoys an enviable reputation among the plumbers of the city. His establishment will be well patronized in the future, and his success in his new business is assured.—
Philadelphia Times

    Arkansas City (Kansas) *Daily Traveler*
    Saturday, June 15, 1889, p3

Cats as Beer Tasters
Malt substitutes Tried on Patient Felines to Determine Their Injurious Qualities

In considering whether corn and other substitutes used in the place of malt in the manufacture of beer were directly injurious to health, Philip Schidrowitz, appearing as an expert before the beer materials' committee of the house of commons, said he had examined the effects of residues of brewing sugars, and the residues of all malt beers on cats. In some of the cases where the residues of brewing sugars were administered to cats, either actual vomiting or retching was caused within from half an hour to an hour, and in two cases slight ataxia was produced.

Seven experiments were conducted with the residues of all-malt beers, the cats having been from 18 to 20 hours without food. The substances were introduced into the stomach in the afternoon of one day, and the next morning all the cats were found to be quite normal, no symptoms of any kind having been observed.

The cat was chosen for these experiments for two reasons, says the *St. Louis Republic*. First, because it is a carnivorous animal, and, secondly, because it is extremely resistant, the latter characteristics rendering it probable that the effects following the administration of the residues were nominal and not maximal. He thought that further investigation in this direction was necessary.

The Yakima (Washington) *Herald*
Thursday, August 4, 1898, p8
Medford (Oregon) *Mail*
Friday, August 19, 1898, p1

Saloon Cat

Strange things may be seen in the larger saloons after midnight. The other morning after the larger part of the crowd had left the saloon, one unfortunate put three chairs in a row and lay down on his side. He was soon asleep, for he had been sitting about two-thirds of the night awaiting the opportunity which had just come to him. The saloon cat jumped on his shoulder and purring in his ear, nestled down and also fell asleep. At length the human sleeper turned on his left side and threw the cat on the floor. Pussy resumed her place on the right shoulder only to be tossed off again half an hour later by her restless human mattress.

Arizona Republic, Phoenix, Arizona
Saturday, February 26, 1898, p5

Feline Pharmacist

An exchange says there is a cat in an uptown drug store whose role in life is a very important and very miserable one. She is used is used by a studious young clerk as an experimental subject. Whenever he concocts a mixture, he administers it to her. She has taken every specimen of pill and powder known to pharmacy, and many known only to the clerk, and she is now practicing on liquids. She has so far imbibed everything successfully. Arsenic makes her lively, strychnine brings on moroseness. After a dose of prussic acid, she is the happiest cat you ever saw. The clerk thinks of trying basement whiskey next, and if that does not kill her, he will give it up.
  Morning Oregonian, Portland, Oregon
  Thursday, April 24, 1873, p3

A Cute Cat that Catches Flies

A man who lives not a hundred miles from this city has a cat that catches flies for a living, or lives to catch flies. It is a tiger-colored kitten about three months old. When a reporter saw the animal bounding about the room, he asked what this is about.

"He's catching flies," explained the owner. "That's what he does the whole day. He has eaten nothing since he was weaned. I can't tell how he came by the habit. We have offered him milk, meat and other food, but he will not touch it. He catches and eats as many as 200 flies some days."

The cat becomes very much excited over his work, and will spring upon a chair or into a window for a

fly. He invariably uses his right paw, and rarely misses his aim.—*Syracuse Herald*
The Galveston (Texas) *Daily News*
Sunday, September 21, 1884, p11

Coyotes and Cats

A man who lives on a ranch in Shirley basin, Wyoming, and had been troubled by field mice and mountain rats, imported several house cats. The coyotes took a liking to cat flesh, and the cats have been killed by the beasts regularly. Four cats disappeared within a few months, but now he has a cat that the coyotes have not captured, although she ventured 200 or 300 yards from the house. The man wants to know why this is so, but the *Forest and Stream* has not answered the question. It has been suggested by a sportsman that it is the same with coyotes as it is with dog fox hounds. When the fox hound gets after a vixen he does not kill or molest her in coming up with her. Since the cat that hasn't been killed is a female, it is fair to suppose that no female coyote has met her yet, but that when a female coyote does come along the puss will be eaten up like the others.
The Anaconda (Montana) *Standard*
Thursday, November 5, 1896, p9

A Trout-Fishing Cat

A recent of this city whose former home was on the margin of Marlette Lake related that his father was the possessor of a large Maltese cat that daily caught trout in the lake in the following manner:

The cat would back down to the edge of the lake, and dropping its tail into water switch it gently from side to side. The ravenous trout, with which the lake is alive, would rise and greedily seize the cat's tail, mistaking it for a monster fly or some new species, and while the trout was endeavoring to swallow it, the cat would suddenly leap landward, landing the fish several feet from the water of the lake, and would then proceed to devour its prey.

The owner of the cat finally trained it to catch fish for the family, as the water company's watchman would not allow any person to fish in the lake, but was not aware of the cat's skill in angling.

The above story is corroborated by several local fishermen—whose veracity has heretofore never been questioned.—*Virginia City Chronicle*

Morning Oregonian, Portland, Oregon
Saturday, October 19, 1889, p15

Suckled by a Dog

Mr. F. Weidner of Mosier is a great hand for pets. About two months ago a dog and a cat gave birth to litters of their respective progeny at about the same time. He drowned all the pups but one, and before long another member of the family had given that away also. About the same time the mother cat was missed. The first time they noticed its absence was by observing the dog nursing the cat family. The kittens were very contented, and while lazily looking with half-closed eyes at the amazed observers, kept their paws moving alternately, unsheathing their sharp little claws each time. This did not seem to disturb the foster mother, who gave the kittens the same attention she formerly did her own offspring—*The Dalles T-M*

The Eugene (Oregon) *Guard*
Tuesday, September 1, 1896, p1

A Cat That Loves the Water

A San Francisco fisherman has a cat that is said to love water as much as other cats love a rug in front of a grate fire. When he goes fishing the cat lies quietly in the boat and does not appear to mind how wet he gets. When the seine with its load of living fishes is hauled in, the cat seizes the largest one, trying to shake it as would a mouse. He does it entirely for sport, as he never attempts to eat the large fish, and lives almost wholly on the smaller ones used for bait.

The Medford (Oregon) *Mail*
Friday, December 7, 1894, p7

An Infatuated Tomcat

Miss Ethel, daughter of D.W. Pease of West Carrollton, is the possessor of a Maltese cat. Early in the spring the cat deserted his place in the house and took up his abode with the chickens, remaining day and night in the chicken yard. He soon formed an attachment for an old black hen, which was reciprocated and the two became inseparable.

Thus, matters went on for some time, when the hen, remembering that the usual season for multiplying and replenishing her species had arrived, selected a nest in the poultry house and made known her intentions in the usual way. She was at once supplied with the necessary eggs and commenced business. This, it was supposed, would end the rather strange flirtation, and Tommy would return to his mat on the porch, but not so. Judge the surprise of the family on going to the poultry house the next day to find that his catship had taken possession of the adjoining nest with the nest egg and was sitting in the most approved fashion.—*Dayton* (Ohio) *Herald*

San Saba (Texas) *County News*
Friday, January 27, 1893, p1

Surrogate Mother

There is a curious thing going on in this town. It was reported yesterday by Dr. Richmond, who says that he never heard of anything like it before. A lady living on South Second Street has a dog of the gentler sex. She also had a cat with a family of very young kittens. The mother cat died or was killed. The dog took possession of the bereft family, and then the most singular incident of this episode occurred. The kittens had been suckling the dog for some time without any substantial benefit. Yesterday they struck milk.

Arizona Republic, Phoenix, Arizona
Tuesday, May 24, 1898, p5

A Cat's Freak.

A cat belonging to a resident of Cameron, Missouri, is nursing a litter of wild rabbits and caring for them with motherly solicitude. Several kittens were born to the cat a week or so ago, but they all died. A neighbor found a nest of very young wild rabbits about the same time and they were put in [the] charge of the cat, with the happy result told.

The Alma (Kansas) *Signal*
Saturday, November 21, 1896, p8

Porcine and Feline

Robert Montgomery has some pets which are a curiosity in their illustration of a strange freak of nature controverting the usual customs of domestic animals. Mr. Montgomery has a pig and a cat that are constant companions, also an old cat with kittens and a small pig. The small pig and kittens nurse, sleep and eat together with the old cat which exercises a motherly care over them.

Arkansas City (Kansas) *Daily Traveler*
Tuesday November 8, 1887, p4

Pet Pals

"One of the most singular friendships I ever saw," said A.R. Mayfield, "is that between a rooster and two cats. The intimacy has lasted two years without a break, bidding fair to continue throughout the lifetime of the fowl and the animals. They are constantly together, the cats following the rooster wherever he goes and he, in turn, calling them up as he would whenever he finds food. When night comes, he roosts upon a feed box, while the cats sleep together in the box. It is a case of pure infatuation, and the three are inseparable—*Astoria Budget*

The Eugene (Oregon) *Guard*
Friday, August 3, 1894, p4

A Peculiar Fight
A Cat Whips a Big Eagle
Escapes Herself from Harm

Sedan, Kan., Sept 21—Arnold Miller, who lives three miles from town, brought in a dead eagle which he says was killed by his cat. The old cat and her kittens were out in the barnyard when the eagle swooped down and grabbed one of the kittens. The cat made a spring at the bird, and a battle royal ensued.

The eagle caught the cat in its claws, but the animal was too quick for the bird and twisted herself around in such a manner that she could bite and scratch the bird's breast. The eagle made a desperate fight, but was unable to loosen the hold the cat had and the result was that it was a dead bird within fifteen minutes from the time it made the attempt to carry off the kitten. The eagle measured six feet from tip to tip, while the cat was an ordinary tabby.

Fort Worth (Texas) *Daily Gazette*
Tuesday, September 22, 1891, p3

Chapter Four

Cats versus Rats (and others)

Cat against mouse is one of the oldest conflicts on earth. That age-old battle between feline and rodent served both an agricultural and a commercial need in the struggle for survival and prosperity. Cats even played a role in protecting the long-distance communication of the time.

With the majority of Americans living on farms for most of the 19th century, agriculture produced grain and perishables that were necessary both for family sustenance and for sale for the funds to purchase the growing number of consumer goods available through mass production. With Chicago mail-order houses putting goods within economic reach of the average family and with the nation's railroad network being able to deliver those goods, average farm families could aspire for more in life than just what they could produce on their own.

Mice and rats, though, through what they consumed and what they spoiled not only took food out of the farm family's mouths but also dollars out of their wallets. Beyond those vermin, other animals, including gophers and squirrels dug up gardens, ate vegetables, damaged fruit trees and created additional challenges to the typical farm family. Consequently, cats became valued partners in rural residents' ability to make ends meet.

Once foodstuffs left the farm or goods the factory, they usually spent some time in warehouses, where rodents again consumed or damaged the products from the hard labors of farm and factory workers, creating further challenges to profitability. Once again, cats came to the rescue providing some protection against rats and mice.

As for long-distance communication, the post office carried the heaviest load through the letters, newspapers and advertising mailers that flooded the postal system. For rats and mice all that paper provided a buffet to satisfy their daily hunger. The problem was so great that most post offices, big and small, kept a cat or two around to combat the rodent damage. The federal government even provided post offices in major cities allocations to pay for cats.

Beyond protecting post office communications, cats provided at least one enterprising editor seeking to improve his profits a way to demonstrate the value of newspaper advertising to a skeptical merchant.

With their natural predatory instincts toward rodents, cats provided an unfathomable economic contribution to the country's prosperity—if not the nation's nighttime rest—and even wound up selling a little advertising on the side.

Cats for Dakota

When it was stated a few days ago that two carloads of cats had been shipped from Iowa to Dakota by an enterprising speculator, and that he was negotiating for another carload, the item presented the appearance of a huge joke; but it seems that it was in real earnest and that the cats are needed there to kill the mice which swarm in the corn and wheat bins and do great damage. The market rate for cats in Iowa is from 50 cents to $1, while quotations in Dakota range from $2.50 to $3, so the cat merchant has a handsome margin.

At the same time, while cats may be much needed in the State which is to be, it does look as though the thing had been overdone. Fancy two, or even three, carloads of felines, squalling and spitting and scratching, their tempers sadly ruffled by confinement in the cars and their eyes shooting sparks, released all at once in Dakota and turned loose in the corn and wheat bins! Why, a blizzard would be a mild infliction in comparison, and a cyclone would be hailed as a welcome relief.

Three carloads of cats! Only imagine the concentration of cussedness which that implies. Fancy the moonlight serenades on the back fences and shed roofs, the number of flying bootjacks and soap dishes, and the amount of Dakotan swear words, which are latent in three carloads of cats. And then the future of Dakota under this new feline dispensation. The very first Legislature will be compelled to enact some sort of a Malthusian law which shall apply to cats in Dakotas, or the situation of that State will be more unbearable than that of

Australia with its rabbit pests.

It will be interesting to watch the Dakota newspapers for a while after the three carloads of cats arrive, see how the people take this extraordinary importation. At first, they will rejoice, in all probability, at the prospect of getting rid of the mice; but after the next generation arrives, and they find cats to the right of them and cats to the left of them, they will possibly sigh for the era of the mice and wish the cats and their progeny back in Iowa.

Just why cats are scarce in Dakota at the present time does not appear. There is scarcely any place in the United States where *felis domestios* is not quite as numerous as is, and why Dakota should be a catless land is somewhat of a mystery. It may be that the cat, which is a very sagacious animal, has grown tired of living under a territorial form of government and has emigrated to places where the people can make their own laws. But this is only idle speculation. The potent fact is the three carloads of cats, and we shall await future developments with much interest and even anxiety

San Francisco Chronicle
Sunday, April 21, 1889, p4
Daily Capital Journal, Salem, Oregon
Wednesday, April 24, 1889, p1
Albany (Oregon) *Daily Democrat*
Thursday, April 25, 1889, p3
Statesman Journal, Salem, Oregon
Wednesday, May 1, 1889, p3
Morning Daily Herald, Albany, Oregon
Friday, May 3, 1889, p3

Squirrel Control

Cats are in demand in Wallowa County [Oregon]. A prairie creek farmer went to Joseph the other day and gathered up every cat in the town, irrespective of age, color, sex or general nativity. He explained to the wondering spectators of his collection that the squirrels are beginning to appear, and that a herd of cats on a ranch is a better investment than poison in the determined war that has to be made on Wallowa's pests. What a pity it is, after all, that Jim Wardner didn't establish that cat ranch over on Puget sound.

*The Eugene (*Oregon*) Guard*
Friday, February 24, 1893, p4

Cats Wanted on the Pacific

A rather novel experiment is being tried on Union Island in the San Joaquin River. This island, like several of its neighbors, was rescued from the tules and the annual floods by levees. An army of Chinamen cleaned out the persistent tule or marsh grass. Since then, it has been put into wheat, and in all, save very wet seasons, has produced royal crops of grain.

For the last two seasons, however, great annoyance has been suffered from the gopher or little ground squirrel, which is found in all parts of California and which is one of the farmer's most dreaded enemies. It destroys grain, kills fruit trees, ravages gardens—in fact combines the destructive properties of the crow, the squirrel and the rabbit, while it is not so large as a good-sized rat.

These pests have increased so rapidly on Union Island that the proprietor of the place has sent out agents all through the San Joaquin and Sacramento valleys to buy cats to keep down the gophers. A bonus of twenty-five cents a head for all good, able-bodied cats, irrespective of sex, has been a big inducement to the small boy, and the agents have already shipped several hundred mousers to the island. One man has extended his wanderings to Oakland, and is reducing the back-fence orchestras of that cheerful city—*Globe-Democrat*

Hutchinson (Kansas) *Herald*

Saturday, March 1, 1884, p4

Thousands Saved by Despised Cats
A Farmer's Happy Experience in the Livermore Valley
No Poison for Gophers
Colonizing Cats Proves a Perfect Remedy
Against Great Evils
Not A Pest in Six Years
Experience That Will Prove of Great Benefit
to Farmers and Ranchers

A new system of protecting potato ranches and orchards from the ravages of squirrels and gophers has been tried in the Livermore Valley and has proved a great success.

The secret of the success is very simple and consists solely of putting to a practical use the common domestic cat.

Although many of the larger class of farmers have resorted to poison, few know or realize the value of a few good cats.

Arthur Small, a well-known farmer in the eastern

part of the county, has experimented for six years and is a great admirer of the common cat, and for good cause.

"Much of the hard-earned profits of the farm go year after year in the expenditure for poison, in order to keep squirrels and gophers from destroying growing crops. Not only in the grain fields is the work of these depredators to be found, but also in the garden, the potato-patch and the orchard. In some districts the rancher is quite unequal to their onslaught, this species of rodent being so numerically strong and destructive that the farmer is deterred from letting his crops ripen into marketable grain, and is driven to the necessity of cutting it all for hay in order to save it.

"I will briefly relate my experience with cats as an aid in place of poison. Several years ago, when I first began farming in my present location, after putting in a small crop for hay, I planted a half-acre or so in potatoes, and also a garden. When the potatoes began to blossom and the garden was in a nice condition, the gophers and squirrels went to work and cleaned up everything in the garden-patch and about half the crop of hay also. The following year I planted the same patch in potatoes and other vegetables, determined to devise some way to save it from the squirrels.

"Again, the garden and crop grew luxuriantly, and while I was contemplating the putting out of poison my observation became centered on the prompt and effective work of a large cat I had on the ranch. She had a couple of active kittens in the barn, and whenever I was around, I saw her engaged in catching gophers and squirrels for the family. As many as ten squirrels were caught daily. Along with the feeding of her kittens, she was frequently waylaid by the dogs, and the squirrel would be taken from her. But she was not discouraged and at once returned and got a fresh carcass, until both the dogs and kittens thrived on her industry.

"I did all I could to encourage the cat, and soon put more to work, and for a long time they have protected me entirely from gophers and squirrels. Although there is unoccupied land around my place, I have never used an ounce of poison in an experience of over six years, and I believe I can show more land cleared up of squirrels than my neighbors, who have poisoned for years. I have no trouble with the cats and no particular system, merely keeping a box to answer for a home for the kittens, keeping them out of the house and only feeding them in winter. With systematic management, the despised house cat can be made of inestimable value to farmers troubled with these pests."

The San Francisco Call
Tuesday, June 16, 1896, p13

Keep Many Cats.

RATS are getting to be a very serious problem with the men who conduct the big warehouses on the business streets near the waterfront, and the person who will invent some efficacious method of driving them out of a building and keeping them out will not only be welcomed with open arms, but will be amply remunerated for his discovery.

These figures may seem exaggerated, but it is a fact

that it costs each warehouse from $50 to $100 a month to repair the damage to goods and building done by the rodents, and the number of the pests seems to be rather on the increase than otherwise.

Thus far cats have been found to be the best means of keeping down the rat crop, and droves of felines are kept in every establishment.

During the day, when the rodents are lying quiet in their retreats, the cats are not particularly noticeable, but after nightfall, when the warehousemen have gone home and darkness reigns in the barn-like structures, fiery eyes peer from every corner, and gaze eagerly and intently at places whence their owners know the prey will come.

Aside from their natural instincts to kill rats, the cats have another reason for hunting assiduously, and that is hunger. Warehousemen want felines that will slaughter steadily and persistently, and have no room for lazy, well-fed cats, so their rat-destroying animals are never fed, but must catch their enemies or starve.

At the Eagle warehouse, 17 and 19 Davis Street, twenty rat-killers are constantly employed weeding out the less cautious of the pests, and these felines destroy an average of fifty rats per day and work seven days in the week. The average of a full-grown and ambitious cat is three rats per day, and when they reach that degree of efficiency they acquire a distinct commercial value, and are carefully protected by their owners.

A few days ago, a member of the Eagle warehouse firm went to look at 500 bales of twine that had been placed in a position where it was supposed they would be safe from rats, and found to his chagrin that almost every bale had been gnawed until it was useless. As the loss falls on the warehouse, he was more than ever angry at the whole rat tribe, and forthwith ordered that an increased supply of the most ferocious cats procurable be purchased. His firm figures its loss from rats $75 per month the year round.

The San Francisco Call
Sunday, September 20, 1896, p23

Warehouse Catastrophe

The stock of cats mentioned a few days ago as being stored at the N.W.S & T. Co's warehouse, have been doing great execution. We were shown this morning, as the result of their labors, about one hundred mice, which they had slaughtered last night. The mice were piled up in windrows ready to be gathered up and taken to burial. The company estimates that the mice, before the advent of cats destroyed from ten to twenty dollars' worth of goods per day.

The Black Hills Daily Times, Deadwood, Dakota Territory, Wednesday, January 30, 1878, p4

Cats on the Pay Roll

Three hundred and odd cats are maintained by the United States government, the cost of their support being carried as a regular item on the accounts of the post office department. They are distributed among about 50 post offices, and their duty is to keep rats and mice from eating postal matter and mail sacks. Their work is of the utmost importance wherever large quantities of mail are collected—as, for example, at the New York post office, where from 2,000 to 3,000 bags of such material are commonly stowed away in the basement. Formerly, great damage was often done by mischievous rodents, which chewed holes in the sacks and thought nothing of boring clear through bags of letters in a night. Troubles of this sort no longer occur, now that the official pussies stand guard. Each city postmaster is allowed from $8 to $40 a year for the keep of his feline staff, sending his estimate for "cat-meat" to Washington at the beginning of each quarter. Care is taken not to feed the animals too high in order that their appetite for live game may be keen. It is laid down as a rule that no meat shall be given when there is a mouse or a rat to be caught.

Cats are kept in all the government buildings at Washington. In that of the state, war and navy departments they are employed not only to protect the priceless papers stored there, but to guard against fire. Twice the war department has been set afire by rats gnawing matches—on one of these occasions in the office of the secretary of war, in the middle of the night. A year ago, the treasury had nine cats, but they made themselves obnoxious and all were given away but two. These are as wild as possible, getting a living by foraging for themselves. Mice are notoriously fond of chewing up money, but they have no chance to get at Uncle Sam's paper cash, which is kept in rooms with iron walls that defy their teeth. Rats occupied the pension office in great numbers while it was in process of building, taking up their residence in the walls and floors as fast as they were put up. Two years ago, four cats were introduced there to guard the records of the old soldiers, and they have driven most of the vermin away. The best rat-killer of the quartet, not long ago, being frightened at something, fell from the second gallery 50 feet to the tiled floor and was killed. The white house has two cats, one a white and black female, kept in the kitchen, and the other a black Tom, which belongs in the stable. Mrs. Harrison had four lovely Maltese pussies, but they all disappeared—stolen, very likely.

But the Capitol is the greatest place in Washington for cats. The huge structure is fairly aswarm with them, and at night they scamper about in troops. Nobody knows how many of them there are, but the watchmen reckon them by scores. They are all vagrants and wild as hawks. In summer they are scattered about the neighborhood to some extent, but in winter they gather within the building. At about 10 o'clock every night they begin a mad racing through the empty corridors, which are made to resound with their cries. The acoustic effects produced are astonishing. Let a single grimalkin lift up his voice in Saturday hall, famous for its echoes, and the silence of the night is broken by a yell like that of a damned soul, as loud as a locomotive whistle. A favorite place for cat concerts is the whispering gallery down below, known as the "crypt," where the feeblest sound is magnified into a roar. Imagine the demoniacal ensemble of half a dozen feline songsters in such a spot!

The Anaconda (Montana) *Standard*
Sunday, November 13, 1892, p9

Post Office Cats

One of Them Who Was
Appropriately Dignified

The post office cat is a very important member of the
federal corps of clerks. In all general post offices,
there are several cats and they every one believe in
civil-service reform. Sixty dollars a year is deemed a
fair appropriation for New York's post office cats'
maintenance, says a writer in the *Boston Herald.* How
the cats feel about it is another matter, but as a usual
thing such small game as rats and mice, which infest
every public building, and their daily allowance of
fresh milk keep them in fine mettle. Our own post
office has a very distinguished black feline known to
the clerks in every department, and respected and
admired from one end of the building to the other.

Not many weeks ago I observed a big cat in a
gray fur coat with dazzling white waistcoat and gray
leggings, sitting on the steps of one of the entrances
to the post office. Hundreds of men were rushing
back and forth, slamming the doors and paying no
heed to Mr. Cat in the corner. All the commotion of
one o'clock in that vicinity did not disturb him in the
least. There was retrospection in his half-closed eyes,
but he did not deign to give an extra twirl to his tail
when his glance met a stranger's gaze, so intent was
he on keeping still. No creature is more nervous than
the cat, yet this one might have come out of a toy
shop for all the hustle and bustle affected him. I shall
never know if he had an appointment with the black

cat within, or whether he was simply waiting for luncheon to be ready. The worst thing about a cat who has cut his wisdom teeth is he won't be communicative. A kitten always gives itself dead away at the first advance.

Abilene (Kansas) *Daily Chronicle*
Saturday, April 16, 1898, p4

People Read Ads
Editor Grady Presented
Incontestable Proof of the Fact

I was reading Wallace Reed's pleasant reminiscence of Henry Grady, and it carried me back to the hard days when Henry was struggling against fate to make his paper a success. The merchants had not then learned the value of advertising, and Henry pleaded in vain for a more liberal patronage. A leading merchant who claimed to be his friend stubbornly declined to give him a big "ad," and said it would be money thrown away, for nobody read them.

"Don't read them!" exclaimed Henry, "don't read them! Well, I will show you."

Next morning's paper contained a short editorial on cats, and told how cat fur had recently come into great demand in fashionable circles in New York, and how the long, coarse hairs were eliminated and the real fur was made into tippets and muffs, and every fashionable lady wore a feline, etc. Not far off in another column was a displayed advertisement that said:

"*Wanted—1,000 cats, for which 50 cents each will be paid.*"

The merchant's name was signed to it.

By noon the cats began to roll in. Small boys, white and black, brought them in baskets and bags. For a while the merchant enjoyed the joke, but soon got tired and went away to dinner.

By the time he returned, the boys and darkies from the suburbs were coming in, and the sidewalk was blockaded. Henry had laughed until he was exhausted, and sat on a window sill across the street, threatened, he said, with a cataleptic fit. Neighboring merchants and their clerks gathered around and laughed and shouted and cried at every new arrival of cats. As fast as the merchant drove off one crowd, another filled their places. He armed himself with a big stick, but at last he closed his doors in sheer despair, and night relieved him from the pressure.

But the next morning the catastrophe was worse. The catalogue was not ended, for the country people had heard the news and brought cats in on their wagons and under their buggy seats, and tied up in cotton baskets like chickens. Henry took his stand nearby and leaned against a telegraph pole for support. He and the folks who loved fun were all there, and, while it was fun to the boys and death to the frogs, it was such a rare and racy joke that the merchant could not get mad, and finally surrendered. He made an appropriate little speech to the crowd and told Henry that if he would promise never to do so any more, he would give him the biggest "ad" he had ever had in his paper. Henry promised, and the "ad" was given—*Atlanta Constitution*

Statesman Journal, Salem, Oregon
Thursday, February 6, 1896, p8

Chapter Five

Cat Burglaries
and Other Crimes

Crime and cats may not go together in the popular imagination except for the term "cat burglar," but felines were involved in activities that had humans committed them would have been considered misdemeanors at best and felonies at worst.

The crimes in question include public intoxication, arson, theft, burglary, assault and even murder. While cats may not have set out to lead a life of crime, circumstances on the frontier made it possible—even likely—that cats would cross the line by accident if not by intent.

Thefts and burglaries are easily explained problems because of cats' natural curiosity or appetite. Missing knickknacks or food could be rationalized as feline fidelity to the tribe's nosey instincts.

Drunkenness even makes sense because saloons stood as social hubs for frontier entertainment and escape, especially among men. Wherever frontiersmen gathered around liquor, their pranks and accidents were inevitable. Saloon patrons may have shared their intoxicants with cats or even spilled beer that the animals licked up. Either way, it led to feline drunkenness and even some cat brawls as reported by the newsprint chroniclers of the time.

Cat arson, assault and murder may be difficult to comprehend with our modern conveniences and sensibilities, but placed in the context of the frontier times they are more understandable. In an era and locale where modern illumination such as gaslights and then electric lights were curiosities, candles and coal-oil lamps and lanterns provided the bulk of lighting. An overturned candle or lamp could quickly engulf a wooden room or building in flames, threatening anyone who might be inside, especially if asleep. Cats knocking over candles and lamps was common enough to receive regular newspaper attention and to perhaps explain the cause behind many inexplicable fires.

While men, women and children might perish in a cat-caused fire, other dangers included cat bites and rabies. Without any antibiotics at the time, any cat bite could be dangerous, even fatal. While rabies or hydrophobia were not confined merely to cats, felines were a common carrier of the viral infection that is transmitted by bites and may take from a day to a year to incubate and attack the central nervous system. Rabies was a painful way of death for which there was no successful treatment on the frontier. Though a vaccine was developed in 1885, it was years before it was commonly available out west.

The news about cat "crimes" was not always negative, as one cat helped its owner solve the theft of a money roll and others awakened household members after the start of unexplained fires. Just as there were good and bad men and women in the Old West, so too were there good kitties and bad kitties.

Detective Cat

The pet cat belonging to Mrs. Lucy Cain, of Hannibal, Missouri, brought a mouse into the parlor recently, and with it a small piece of paper money. Mrs. Cain thought nothing about the occurrence until one day last week, when she discovered that a roll of bills was missing from her bureau drawer. Then she put two and two together, and began a vigorous search of the premises. The missing bills were finally unearthed in a corner of the cellar, where a colony of mice had made a nest of them.

The Dallas (Texas) *Daily Herald*
Monday, March 28, 1887, p5

Drunken Cats in a Fight

A most exciting cat fight occurred last week in the back room of N. Bergmeyer's saloon. Thirteen cats met there, presumably to discuss plans by which they could most effectually disturb midnight slumbers, when, in the midst of a discussion, and while a large tomcat was making an impassioned address, a dispute arose and the fun began. Fur flew and a din was made that aroused the town. It was dangerous to attempt to quell the riot, as the cats seemed perfectly wild.

After a few minutes they ceased from sheer exhaustion, and three cats lay stone dead, the others staggering off to their various homes. They presented such an appearance of intoxication that George Motes, the barber, made an investigation and found that the cats had been drinking beer which had been left in a keg in a corner of the room. He determined to watch the keg, and late that evening saw a cat walk into the room, slyly creep to the keg, where it drank until hilarious. This story may appear incredible, but it is a fact, nevertheless—*Greenup* (Kentucky) *Democrat*

Statesman Journal, Salem, Oregon
Sunday, July 16, 1899, p6

A Cat That Drinks
A Confirmed Old Toper
That Loves Beer.

There is a dog in this city, says the *Phenix* (cq) *Republican*, who is a habitual drunkard, but the canine has a rival in a cat belonging to a saloonkeeper.

Tabby was taught to relish a mug of beer. The saloonkeeper poured beer in small quantities into a saucer of milk and gradually increased the portion of beer and decreased the amount of milk. This was kept up daily until Tabby was drinking beer straight. The cat has now developed into a regular old toper, and if allowed will drink beer until unable to walk.

It is almost a daily occurrence now to see the cat staggering blindly around the saloon. When Tabby thinks it's time for another drink, she scratches the refrigerator with her claws to attract the attention of the bartender, and if that individual refuses to give any more she will sulk off and will not return until in a respectable condition of sobriety.

The other day the cat had a narrow escape from finding the grave ready for all drunkards. The bartender opened the refrigerator door and did not observe Tabby sneaking in. He closed the door and did not have occasion to open it for several hours. When he did so, he recoiled at the sight of Tabby standing on her four legs and staring with wide open eyes that did not blink. She was taken out and found to be almost frozen solid. She could not move a muscle and was to all appearances dead. It took some time for her to thaw but she was given all the beer she could possibly drink to atone for the imprisonment in the ice box.

Tombstone (Arizona) *Prospector*
Saturday, October 17, 1896, p4

It Was the Cat
A Milkman Relates Experiences and Tells a Pleasant Little story

"Don't you know that women are the greatest 'kickers' on earth?" said a well-known milkman to a *Bee* representative a few days since. The conversation was not regarding Lydia Thompson or other burlesque artists, but the dispenser of lacteal fluid was discoursing regarding his everyday experience.

"You have no idea how many complaints and growls I hear," he continued, "and if I don't get 'blowed up' by fifty different women during a day I can't sleep at night. One standing complaint with many of them is that the milk I serve sours quicker than it should. Of course, I know that the reason the milk turns is that the tins or other vessels in which it is placed are not thoroughly clean, but I can't say so. The women would be mortally insulted. Then, again, they complain that I don't give them sour milk enough, and they make frequent allusions to someone who enjoyed their patronage in the past, telling how handsomely they were treated by Smith, or Jones, or some other milkman who was probably hurried to their final reward by their exactions. The most general complaint, however, is in regard to measurements, and there seem to be scores of women who are imbued with the idea that they are being swindled by the milkman.

The most memorable experience of this kind I ever had was with a woman down on N Street. She was constantly complaining that I did not give her good measure, notwithstanding I was unusually careful at her place and used to pour in a little extra milk to make sure. She always left a lard can on the front door step, covered with a lid much too large for the can. Well, one morning after I had left her milk, I was driving back up the street and happened to glance toward where she left her milk can. I saw a large cat approaching the milk, and became interested in a moment. I stopped the wagon and watched the cat.

Well, sir, that infernal cat went right up to the milk can, took the ring in the center of the lid in his mouth, lifting the cover off and setting it on the step.

Then his catship went for the milk, and lapped, and lapped, and lapped, and I sat there and watched. The cat kept up his lick until his sides stuck out, and then he picked up the cover, put it back on the milk can, and ambled under the house, presumably to take a snooze.

"When I went around on the, afternoon delivery, I told the woman what I had seen. She replied, 'Y-e-s,' in a doubtful sort of way, and I saw in a minute that she thought I was lying. That riled me, but when the next afternoon the woman smiled sarcastically and said, 'I guess that cat was around again this morning,' it made me crazy. I came up town and bought a small shelf and had it put up in front of the house at my own expense. The milk can has been there since, and while I don't know whether the woman ever believed about the cat, I know she doesn't growl any more about short measurement."

"What became of that talented cat?" inquired the reporter.

"I don't know," replied the milkman, musingly, "but from the complaints I hear I shouldn't wonder but what that darned cat is following me around on my route, just for revenge and is repeating that trick, which was a little the cunningest thing I ever [did] see."—*Sacramento Bee*
Oakland (California) *Tribune*
Friday, February 10, 1888, p6

Bird Palls

House cats are numerous around deserted logging camps and do more in destroying game birds than all

other causes combined. Young coveys of pheasants, grouse and quail are rapidly exterminated, and in view of this fact, it is no wonder that game birds are getting scarcer. A hunter should never miss an opportunity to shoot a house cat when he finds it running wild in the woods.—*Coos Bay News*
The Eugene (Oregon) *Guard*
Wednesday, December 20, 1893, p3

Faking and Entering

Quite an excitement was caused in the west end one night last week by what was supposed to be burglars attempting to gain an entrance through a window, but investigation proved the intruder to be the family cat scratching on the window screen. The man of the house, who secured the services of a neighbor or two to help rout the burglar, has had to buy many cigars to quiet the friends who were informed of his display of bravery.
Lincoln County Tribune, North Platte, Nebraska
Wednesday, November 14, 1894, p3

Cat Fight!

A cat fight of no mean dimensions is reported from the Cow creek neighborhood that is nothing if not sensational. The correspondent says: On Sunday night about midnight, I heard a sound like the rushing of a mighty wind, commingled with the noise of many waters, and the modulations of various and sundry meows of a cat at my window. Armed with an iron poker I ventured forth in search of his catship.

As soon as I got in the neighborhood of where I thought I heard the noise, I saw a large light brindle cat weighing about 24 pounds. How the animal got into my house is a mystery to me as all my doors were locked and my windows pinned down, but it was on the inside all the same, and when I approached an awful fight ensued—between me and the cat. I struck it over the head with the iron poker with all my strength but without effect. I then drew my 38-caliber from my hip pocket and shot the savage beast twice, through the back and also in the head, but apparently without effect.

Up to this time I had got decidedly the worst of the fight, so I retreated, and called a neighbor, Boon Phelps, who came to my assistance with a shotgun and then we made short order of it. Strange to say, not a single shot took effect in the wall or floor of the building; all lodged in the body of the cat. It is a great puzzle to myself and all my neighbors how the animal got in the house and where he came from. This is a true tale.—Wm. Harris.

About the only solution we are able to offer to the above is that, maybe it will turn out like the celebrated "Lincoln cat fight"—just more cats. [Editor]

(Editor's Note: Perhaps a reference to the Abraham Lincoln quote: No matter how much cats fight, there always seem to be plenty of kittens.)

The Weekly Chieftain, Vinita, Oklahoma
Thursday, February 4, 1897, p3

It Was the Cat

C.H. Lee, the civil engineer, was awakened from pleasant dreams on Sunday night by some sort of noise, he don't know exactly what. On looking towards the open window of his room, he noticed, in the darkness, some kind of a dark object, which he could not account for. He went to the window and attempted to pull the object, which appeared like a piece of cloth. To his surprise, he found that it was his trousers and that some sort of live attachment was at the other end. He made a further investigation, and discovered that it was a cat, which was pulling them out—a regular four-legged feline.

Weekly Journal-Miner, Prescott, Arizona
Wednesday, August 12, 1896, p3

A Small Residence Burned
The Cat That Did the Mischief

Fort Smith, Ark., March 9—The residence of George Parker was destroyed by fire today. The fire was caused by a cat knocking a can of coal oil off a shelf which fell on the stove. Oil was spilt on Mrs. Parker's clothing, which caught fire and she was badly burned and her husband slightly burned with endeavoring to extinguish her clothing. The loss was about seven hundred dollars; no insurance.

Fort Worth (Texas) *Daily Gazette*
Monday, March 10, 1884, p2

Special Delivery!

Yesterday Charles Wier's meat wagon was smashed up. The driver hitched up the team and just as he was starting out of the alley, a cat ran under the horses' feet and scared them. They started to run and ran across Seventh Avenue and in going up the alley, collided with a post. The horses broke loose from the wagon, but were caught near the Gladstone. They were not injured. The wagon was badly broken, and the driver injured his leg slightly.

Arkansas City (Kansas) *Daily Traveler*
Wednesday, January 2, 1889 p8

Plan Gone Wrong

A man near New Kirk, Oklahoma Territory, took his neighbor's cat, saturated its tail in kerosene and set it on fire, thinking it would run home and burn the neighbors out. Instead, it turned and jumped into the torturer's own barn and burned it down. *The cat came back* sure enough.

The Indian Advocate, Sacred Heart, Oklahoma
Wednesday, July 1, 1896, p15

Playing with Matches

A cat came near being the destruction of the Gregory house lately. The cat has been a pet for many years and in the capacity of pet has taken liberties not accorded to the average cat. Among these liberties was the privilege of "snooping" around. The other day the cat was investigating the contents of a shelf in an unoccupied room. She knocked a box of matches on the floor and the jar was sufficient to ignite them. Someone passing along the hall was attracted by the smell of burning cloth and smoke exuding from the door. A hole three feet in diameter had been burned in the carpet and the flames had begun to eat into the woodwork of the floor. If this discovery had been delayed five minutes or perhaps only one minute, that section of Phoenix would have been a blackened ruin.

Arizona Republic, Phoenix, Arizona
Wednesday, December 18, 1897, p5

Santa Cruz Residence Burned

SANTA CRUZ, Dec. 2—The residence of A.S. Bias was destroyed by fire today. The family barely escaped with their lives. Bias's hair was burned off in making his escape. The fire was caused by a cat upsetting a lamp. Loss, $1,500, with small insurance.

The Record-Union, Sacramento, California
Friday, December 3, 1897, p8

Rough on the Cat

While the little daughters of Councilman Wm. Getchell were in the parlor enjoying a pleasant evening with their friends, the house cat was having a rather warm time in the kitchen. The cat had crawled in the oven of the cook stove, and the little girls not knowing it was in there closed the oven door and started a fire. In the course of half an hour they returned to the kitchen to be greeted by a strong smell of burning hair. Upon investigation the cat was found to be baked to a nice brown, and, though dead, was "a very warm thing."

La Grande (Oregon) *Observer*
Tuesday, April 19, 1898, p3

Nothing to See Here

If your chicks are missing and there is a mystery about their disappearance it might do no harm to interview the cat. A chicken-killing cat is the most demure hypocrite on earth and will look so innocent and satisfied with herself that it seems almost wicked to doubt her, but a good many times she is the guilty one.

Ranche and Range, Yakima, Washington
Thursday, September 2, 1897, p13

The Cat Did It *(Again)*

Whitesboro, Tex., Feb. 11—J.M. Brooks' residence, a few miles southwest of town, was burned on the night of the 9th, caused by a cat upsetting the lamp. The flames spread so rapidly that only a few articles of bedding and a bureau were saved. The house and contents were valued at about $1,500 and insured in the Phoenix of Hartford for $1,100.

Fort Worth (Texas) *Daily Gazette*
Friday, February 12, 1886, p5

Two Burglaries

They Were Both Committed
on Monday Night Last

Since the recent demonstration against thugs, thieves and footpads there have been very few crimes committed in the city, but it looks as if some of the criminal elements were coming back to do business at the old stand.

On Monday night two places were broken into and robbed—the store of W. Brome at Eighth and O streets and another in the southern part of the city kept by a man named Bogart.

From Brome's store a quantity of groceries, tobacco, bread, cakes, nuts, etc., were carried off, but nothing of great value. The proprietor and his wife live in the rear of the store, and Mrs. Brome was awakened by the noise made by the burglars, but thought it was made by some cats in the backyard. One of the burglars was there, however, and when Mrs. Brome was heard opening the door he ran around to the front and warned his confederates.

At Bogart's a window was smashed in and a quantity of stuff stolen.

Mr. Brome stated yesterday that both cases were promptly reported to the police, and he was surprised to find the facts had not been given to the press. He thinks if they had been, some outsider might have discovered the thieves with their plunder.

The Record-Union, Sacramento, California
Thursday, March 14, 1895, p4

Tragic Result

We often hear of cats getting into all kinds of mischief, but here is an extraordinary case: near Fredericksburg, a few days ago, a cat killed a colored baby only a few days old.

Brenham (Texas) *Weekly Banner*
Friday, April 5, 1878, p1

Accidentally Killed

LaGrange, Tex., Dec. 31—A farmer named C. D. Roscher, who lives near Cedar, five miles from here, accidentally killed himself. He intended to kill a cat with a .32-caliber rifle. The trigger of the weapon caught on something and caused it to fire, the ball passing through Roscher's head, killing him instantly. He leaves a family.

The Bryan (Texas) *Daily Eagle*
Friday, January 1, 1897, p1

What's Cooking?

A lady at Galveston recently, without knowing it, shut her favorite cat up in the stove and made a fire. When the stove began to get hot Tom began to yell, and hearing him she let him out. The cat died.

Shiner (Texas) *Gazette*
Thursday, December 28, 1893, p3

Texas News Items

Bell County: On Monday, while Mr. Will Moore and family were at breakfast, the cries of the house cat were heard in the front room, and when Mr. Moore's young son went to open the door to let it out, he found the room in a blaze. Mr. Moore came speedily to the rescue and found the bed and carpet on fire and the walls about to catch. By heroic efforts the fire was put out by himself and some neighbors."—
Belton Journal
  The Galveston (Texas) *Daily News*
  Wednesday, November 22, 1882, p4

Feline Houdini

The other day, in North San Juan, the owner of a chicken-stealing cat gave 25 cents to a boy to drown it. The cat was put in a sack, and the mouth of the sack tied tightly with a strong cord. The boy took the bag to a ditch, put it under a waterfall made by the water pouring from a sluice-box, and left it to its fate. The next morning the gentleman found the cat in its accustomed place by the stove.
  The Record-Union, Sacramento, California
  Friday, August 27, 1880, p1

Combination of Circumstances

The window of a dentist's office came down and caught a cat by the tail while he was out, and fourteen people who would have waited for his return, on going upstairs and hearing the cat's voice decided to go home and stand the pain of the toothache.— [Exchange]

The Record-Union, Sacramento, California
Wednesday, October 3, 1883, p8

Pacific Coast Items

The little five-year-old girl of H.S. Rowe of Seattle, W.T., was shot by her mother Saturday. Mrs. Rowe wished to kill a cat. She shot the feline and the ball struck the wall and, glancing from its course, hit the child above the right groin. The child is doing well.

The Record-Union, Sacramento, California
Monday, July 9, 1883, p1

Rabid Cat

Marshall, Tex., July 1—A cat supposed to be rabid attacked Col. F.B. Sexton on the pavement, tearing his pants but failing to lacerate the skin. It was a hard matter to pull and beat the animal away.

The Galveston (Texas) *Daily News*
Monday, July 3, 1893, p9

Laundry Losses

A cat owned by a farmer who lives near Norwich, Connecticut, has developed a fancy for stealing clothes-pins. While the animal is never known to touch clothes-pins of its owner, it brings home all it can find lying loose in the neighbors' yards. Within the last three months twenty-eight dozen have been brought home in this way.

The Record-Union, Sacramento, California
Saturday, February 2, 1889, p7

A Fatal Cat Bite

Oklahoma City, Okla., Oct. 12—J.A. Eldridge, a farmer, living on a claim between Moore and Norman, died on Tuesday night of hydrophobia, having suffered for a week or ten days with all the horrible delusions and terrible spasms of that dreadful disease.

A cat bit him ten days or two weeks ago. He began to feel badly. The disease developed rapidly, and in a short time he was a raving maniac, frothing at the mouth, scratching and biting like a cat, mewing and spitting. Although weak, it took several strong men to hold him in bed and finally they had to strap him to the bed.

His principal delusion was that he was fighting a cat, and his struggles and cries were terrible and pitiful.

The Galveston (Texas) *Daily News*
Friday, October 13, 1893, p2

Facts of Interest

During 1881, 28 dogs, 83 cats, 567 chipmunks, 567 black mice, 1,298 rats, 28 snakes, 5 muskrats and 15 moles were caught in Greenwood Cemetery by a man employed there as a trapper. He is thinning the moles out, and they were the most destructive of the many animal pests with which Greenwood abounded.

Nevada State Journal, Reno, Nevada
Friday, July 11, 1884, p1

A Cat and Dog Fire

Seattle, Wash., Oct. 27—F. Golding went into a dark room to get some paint. He had a lamp with him and was followed by a dog. A cat came in and was chased by the dog. They overturned the lamp and set fire to the paint. Before the fire was put out, $2,000 damage was done to the building.

Eugene (Oregon) *Guard*
Saturday, October 27, 1894, p1

A Cat Roasted

We are informed that a big cat was roasted in a cook stove oven in the southeastern portion of the city yesterday, accidentally. It appears that the feline has been in the habit of resting in the oven of the stove, and yesterday the door became closed some way and a hot fire was built in the furnace and the cat was badly roasted before he was rescued.

Eugene (Oregon) *Guard*
Tuesday, July 7, 1896, p4

Life's Woes

A Eugene man heard burglars on his roof. He bravely investigated matters and found a cat making the burglarious noise. Thus, a great many troubles in life prove to be merely cats.—*Albany Democrat*

Eugene (Oregon) *Guard*
Friday, August 7, 1896, p4

Cat Prevents Suicide

A Washington woman who started to jump into the Columbia River to drown herself suddenly remembered that she had left the cat in the pantry, and hurried back home. She afterward said: "The idea of my struggling in the water and thinking that that cat was a licking the cream off of my milk in the pantry at that minute was more than I could bear!"

Lincoln County Leader, Toledo, Oregon
Thursday, December 28, 1893, p1

Demise by Cat

The following is an exact copy of a coroner's jury verdict in a New Mexican town: "We, the jury, find that the deceased came to his death by a shot accidentally went off by himself by killing a cat by shooting the same and when she was not dead instantly by striking the cat with the breach of the gun and the load discharged itself."

Morning Oregonian, Portland, Oregon
Thursday, July 29, 1875, p1

Outwitted by Cat

"It was evening. Three of them were killing a cat.
One of them held a lantern, another held the cat, and
the third jammed the pistol into the cat's ear, and
fired, shooting the man in the hand who held the cat,
and the one with the lantern was wounded in the arm.
The cat left when it saw how matters stood, and that
ill-feeling was being engendered."

The New Northwest, Portland, Oregon
Friday, September 8, 1876, p3

The Cat Came Back

A large Maltese cat, the property of Judge Osbourne,
who lives on Howard Avenue, near Howell Street, has
stirred the entire neighborhood to a high state of
excitement by making nightly raids on chicken coups.
One man, Mr. Luther, is mourning the killing by the
cat of 26 valuable hens, while other neighbors have
reported smaller losses. Mr. Osbourne will not kill
the cat or pay for the chickens. The men who have
had their poultry killed have decided to form a
vigilant (cq) committee and catch the cat, and then
another mysterious disappearance will be reported.

The Seattle (Washington) *Star*
Friday, July 28, 1899, p3

Chapter Six

Cat~~tle~~ Drives

As predictable as a hangover after an all-night bender, cats followed prospectors to mining bonanzas across the West once entrepreneurs realized herding cats—difficult as it may have been— was much easier than extracting ore from the stubborn earth.

Though cats created headaches in towns where they proliferated because of their rambunctious nighttime noisemaking, they provided a cure-all for mining towns where rats and mice flourished amidst the detritus and filth of the typical mining operation.

For the poor man without the capital required for big-time, industrial mining, cat wrangling offered a high return on a small investment. In communities where cats proliferated, they were available for the taking—if a fellow could catch them. In boomtowns where they were needed, felines brought exorbitant prices to combat the rodent problem.

From California boomtowns in 1849 to the Yukon

in 1899, cats became as necessary as picks, shovels, sluice boxes and grub to counter the millions of rodents that overran roughhewn communities on the fringe of civilization and civility. A mineral boom ultimately kicked off a cat boom.

The most famous cat drive in Old West history was the "house cats for cat houses" load delivered in June 1876 by Phatty Thompson to "the girls of the gulch," as local prostitutes were called by Deadwood's *Pioneer-Times*. Thompson had paid Cheyenne, Wyoming, boys a few cents for each cat they caught, then freighted the kitties to Deadwood to sell to "the lonely dancehall girls," who by some accounts had requested them for companionship. Thompson sold the cats to the gals and other Deadwood denizens for up to a hundred and fifty times what he had paid for them. Every dollar Thompson received for his cat commerce was the equivalent of $27.85 in 2022 dollars.

From Sutter's Mill to the Klondike rushes, felines followed, generally against their will. The following selections are listed chronologically by the date of the rush rather than the date of the publication as some accounts are from pioneer recollections. While cats in that era were generally treated like the animals they were without the sensitivity of the modern perspective, attitudes were evolving, raising the ire of some frontiersmen. The *Black Hills Weekly Pioneer* in 1880 printed a tongue-in-cheek account of changing attitudes and criticizing Henry Bergh, who founded the American Society for the Prevention of Cruelty to Animals (ASPCA) in 1866, formalizing a movement for better treatment of animals, including cats, much to the chagrin of the *Weekly Pioneer* author.

Though Bergh was headquartered in New York and confined most of his direct efforts against animal cruelty to the northeast, he understood that his crusade was useless without publicity so he invited newspaper reporters to accompany him. Through the resulting news accounts and the newspaper exchange program where the publications shared and re-printed each other's stories, Bergh after the Civil War became well-known across the country

The skeptical opinion of Bergh by the Black Hills journalist quoted in this chapter was shared by newspapers across the country, often with a particular disdain for felines. "The protection of cats," wrote an editor in *Spirit of the Times*, a New York City-based national weekly, "should be the lowest grade of animals to which [Bergh] should give his humane attention." *Spirit of the Times* identified itself as a "chronicle of the turf, agriculture, field sports, literature and the stage."

Cats, it seems, were no more valued in the big city than they were in the mining boomtowns of the American West. Even so, whether loved or loathed, cats and their exploits consistently appeared in ink in the columns of frontier newspapers.

Grandkittens of the Twenty-Seventh Great

James Whitaker, a reputable citizen of Camptonville, California, has a "granny" cat which crossed the plains with him in '49. She was a kitten then and is, therefore, nearly thirty-four years old. Martha Washington is the cat's name. It is estimated that Martha has between 4,000 and 5,000 descendants,

reaching to grandkittens of the twenty-seventh great.
The Bismarck (North Dakota) *Tribune*
Friday, March 23, 1883, p7

From Tacks and Cats
How Two Snug Fortunes
Were Acquired in Early Days

"The first 'corner' on record in California," said a pioneer yesterday, "was that made by a Boston man in 1849.

"He observed that tacks were used in all mining and building operations. Thinking he saw a chance to make a turn, he bought all the tacks in the city and all those to arrive. Soon there was a round demand for tacks, and our Boston man sold his at their weight in gold, ounce for ounce, and returned home with a fortune.

"Another corner was made by a Virginia negro, Peter Briggs. He arrived in Los Angeles in 1849 as the servant of Captain A. J. Smith of the dragoons, afterward, during the war, commander of the Sixteenth Army Corps.

"Peter was known to the Americans in Los Angeles as the Black Democrat, and the Mexicans called him 'Don Pedro.'

"He engaged in speculation, and finally set up a barbershop, the only one in the village. But his big strop was the corner in cats.

"San Francisco was overrun with rats in those days and short on cats. The reverse was the case in Los Angeles.

"Peter laid traps for the cats, and every night

would capture a batch of them. He secured enough to make a schooner cargo and brought them to San Francisco, where they were sold at from $5 to $25 each, netting him a modest fortune.

"But Peter could not stand prosperity, and lost his cornered fortune at the old El Dorado gambling-house."

The San Francisco Call
Sunday, September 25, 1892, p14
Muskogee (Oklahoma) *Phoenix*
Thursday, November 3, 1892, p6

A Corner in Cats

"You may talk about your wheat corners," said the old '49er, "but they don't compare with the corner in cats a man got up in California in the early days. San Francisco at that period [1849] was a tumbledown village of pine boards built on a marsh. The place was overrun with large, long-tailed, voracious rats which made life a burden to the inhabitants. We who lived there then weren't particularly delicate in our personal tastes, but when it came to losing toes and fingers while we slept, we got right up and objected to the limit of our vocabularies. There were a few cats in the town, of course, but they were kept too busy to increase any, and their daily walks were so full of excitement that they didn't live long. Well, it finally got to be a case of too bad, and cats were quoted on the bourse [market] at fifty dollars per ordinary cat.

"Experienced cats and cats with records brought higher prices. Down in the southern part of the state, they had more cats than they knew what to do with.

A sharp chap in Los Angeles heard about the state of affairs in 'Frisco, and he goes and borrows all the money he can and then buys up every cat south of Tehachapi at four for one dollar. Then he loads Cap Haley's *Sea Bird* with 'em, brings 'em up to our town and auctions them off. He gets as high as $75 apiece, and clears several thousand dollars. The cats did the business, too, and inside of six weeks there was not a solitary rat in San Francisco. But we had a time afterward getting rid of the cats."—*Chicago Post*
    The Capital Journal, Salem, Oregon
    Tuesday, October 6, 1891, p4

The Cat Trade in California

The San Francisco correspondent of the *New York Journal of Commerce*, in his letter of the first of April, says:

"The steamer *Ohio*, on her last trip from San Diego, brought into port an importation of "Cats," 96 in number. They cost at the place of embarkation about 50 cents a head, and sell here from ten to twenty dollars each, according to size, sex and general condition. A passenger on board the steamer told me that they had a very musical time of it. This is truly a novel article of traffic, but one of the fruits of the coast trade, just opening on the Pacific by our numerous little steamers, which run regularly every week up and down the coast."
    The Arkansas Banner, Little Rock, Arkansas
    Tuesday, June 3, 1851, p3

A Western Whittington and his Cats

Here comes a story for you which sounds almost like an out-West fairy tale, but I am told that it is strictly true: "During the first days of 'Pike's Peak,' [1858] when that country was being occupied by mining prospectors, their cabins were overrun with rats—not your domesticated, house-mice and rats of an old civilized community, but rats—large, ravenous rats— with teeth and digestive apparatus capable of managing anything from a tough old boot to a dainty piece of breakfast bacon.

"This state of affairs came to the knowledge of a thrifty Dutchman, poor, but willing to earn a bright dollar if the way was only pointed out, and roused his dormant ideas to take advantage of the rat nuisance and profit thereby. The Dutchman secured a yoke of oxen, rigged a prairie-schooner with three stories, and filled the same with good cats, which his neighbors were glad to be rid of. With this outfit he started across the plains for Pike's Peak, a tedious journey of some 600 miles. This, with scant supplies of game, prepared the cats for any encounter with their victims.

"Their arrival spread joy among the householders, and everything was set aside to purchase cats. When the stock of our worthy Dutchman had been speedily converted into gold-dust, he sold his team, returned on foot across the desert plains to Omaha with over $1,500, and bought a farm nearby. But the climax of this venture was attained when his faithful oxen strayed back to him."— in *St. Nicholas.*

The Evening Kansan, Newton, Kansas
Thursday, December 31, 1891, p4, and Friday, February 26, 1892, p4

The Record-Union, Sacramento, California
Monday, January 18, 1892, p1

A Market for Cats

Shortly after the discovery of the Comstock mine, an old gentleman was unable to meet [a] mortgage of $1,500 on his place on Mormon Island [California]. A stranger, stopping at his door, saw several pretty kittens playing in the yard. He said: "Those cats, if you had them on the Comstock, would bring you $20 apiece." The old man saddled his horse, and for the next fortnight rode from house to house, farm to farm, and village to village, begging and buying cats. He got 500, and sold them on the Comstock mine, and after he had paid off his mortgage and put in bank $500 clear, he told his neighbors why he had wanted cats. They no longer deemed him crazy on cats.

Arizona Daily Star, Tucson, Arizona
Saturday, September 6, 1884, p1

Of the Territory at Large

He (Colonel Poston of the *San Francisco Bulletin* on California) says: The variety of climate is so great that at Fort Yuma, its southwestern corner, the mercury ranges higher than any other military post in the United States, and at Fort Defiance, its northeastern corner, five soldiers on guard were frozen to death a few years ago. The present Territory is composed of three great sections, each inaccessible to the other, and all of them to the balance of the world.

The section south of the Gila—western, part desert; central, mining and farming; eastern, mining, farming and grazing; the section of the Colorado, reaching from near the Gulf of California to the Great Utah Basin, commercial and mining. The section north of the Gila, the interior, centering around the capital, is the finest climate of all, the best country to live in—plenty of grass, considerable arable land, and more mines than any other part of the Territory explored. In this section families are coming in with the great wave of emigration from the Western States, and here will build them houses as permanent as the granite mountains which surround them. They bring wagons, oxen, cows, horses, mules, dogs, cats, and, over and above all, women, the greatest refining institution ever in a mining country. The virginity of the country, the exhilaration of the atmosphere, and the bright hopes of the future seem to pervade every soul. I have not seen a gloomy or unhappy man in that interior section.

Arizona Miner, Fort Whipple, Arizona
Wednesday, September 21, 1864, p2

News from Boise

The miners in Bannock district have refused to lay over their claims, and all claims not worked at least one day in each week are liable to be jumped. Cats and chickens are in great demand at Boise. A respectable "tabby" readily commands $10; chickens are quoted at $36 per dozen.—*Boise News*

Weekly Oregon Statesman, Salem, Oregon
Monday, October 12, 1863, p3

Cats from Cheyenne

The girls of the gulch have received cats from Cheyenne.

Phatty Thompson brought in a load of the feline pets and is said to have cleared a thousand dollars from their sale to the lonely dancehall girls. He bought the cats for two bits apiece, sold them in the gulch for prices that ranged from $10 to $40 apiece. After an hour of haggling, only a few cats were left. They were unsalable because of the fighting they had done so Phatty offered them at reduced rates and had plenty of takers.

Black Hills Weekly Pioneer, Deadwood, South Dakota, Thursday, June 8, 1876, p1

Cats
(Letter to the Editor)

We have sometimes wondered why some enterprising, speculative individual had not yet thought of importing a load of cats to the Black Hills. An ordinary freight wagon could be partitioned off so as to carry with ease and safety two hundred cats. These cats could be obtained with little or no cost in any of the towns along the Missouri river, and they would find a ready market here at an average price of ten dollars each. The man who has the sagacity and nerve to bring the load of cats into the Black Hills can lay claim to having struck a rich feline lode.— *Champion.*

Mr. Champion: You are behind the times. That enterprising individual imported a load of cats last fall, that were auctioneered here to the highest bidder on Main Street. You say these cats could be procured in any town along the Missouri River. Ah, you have friends there in the cat trade, have you? Why not say that they could be procured in Denver, San Francisco, or New York? It is evident, sir, that you have a corner on these cats, or else you have an interest in some bootjack manufactory.

The Black Hills Daily Times, Deadwood, South Dakota, Monday, June 11, 1877, p1

The First Cat

D.C. Walker, now a flourishing farmer in Spearfish, brought the first cat to the Hills in 1876. He brought a double-deck wagon-load of mousers, which he sold at one-half ounce of gold dust per cat.

Black Hills Weekly Pioneer, Deadwood, South Dakota, Saturday, February 7, 1880, p4

Cat Cargo

A visitor to the city at the present time would hardly credit the fact that the most profitable cargo of livestock ever brought to the Hills, consisted of felines. It was in '76; and the genius who conceived the brilliant idea claimed Nebraska as his home. He brought in a mixed cargo of all ages, sexes, previous conditions of servitude, and breed, from the excellent Maltese mouser, to the bright coated Angora, all of which found ready sale at prices ranging from ten to twenty dollars per cat.

Four years have passed; the importation has multiplied until now the city favorably compares with any in the east as regards the abundance of midnight disturbers. In fact, cats are becoming a positive nuisance, and our condition akin to that of New York where the people are waging a war of extermination, and to such an extent as to cause the brute-itarian [Henry] Bergh to raise his voice in denunciation of the manner in which felines are massacred. He says if the city of New York wishes to decrease the stock of cats now on hand, it must do so by drowning them in a respectable and delicate way, or he will bring down the wrath of the law upon any one who gets rid of a black, white, yellow or brindle cat in a manner otherwise than he has dictated. The tyrannical action taken by Bergh in the cat question is a blow struck at the privileges vouchsafed to every American citizen, and may yet cause the republic to tremble on its foundations.

The time when a man could crawl along the back gallery in his night shirt, and tear a vociferous cat into fragments with a double-barrel shotgun has passed away.

The right that each and every American citizen had to chase one out of the kitchen and pulverize his active form with a cobblestone as he was in the act of scooting over the back fence is now no more. It has become a matter of history, and will be looked back to years hence by the coming generation as a privilege enjoyed by their fathers, and which through the fanaticism of one man has been denied to them.

Bergh's desire to drown the cats has called forth the ire of all the old maids throughout the country, whose solitary existence is only cheered by the affectionate purring of their idolized Tabbies. Shall the home of each of these fossilized specimens of female celibacy be made desolate by the cruel taking off of her cherished pet? Shall the faithful cat, who has mewed its love and rubbed its fur against the cheek never contaminated by the beard of man, be plucked from her hearthstone and consigned to a watery grave? No, let Marian remain with her mistress and be the recipient of that wealth of love which no man seemed anxious to win.

Black Hills Weekly Pioneer, Deadwood, South Dakota, Saturday, October 23, 1880, p1

Meow-meow-oh

Thomas Sheffery of Orleans, Neb., has a cat farm. He raises cats and ships them by the car load to Denver, where those of the male gender sell as high as $5 each.

Great Falls (Montana) *Tribune*
Saturday, December 5, 1885, p1
The Dakota Huronite, Huron, South Dakota
Thursday, December 17, 1885, p7

Kitty Litters

Kansas seems to have developed a new industry—supplying new Colorado towns overrun by rats with cats. A thousand tom cats are being collected by the firm of Humphrey & Humphrey of Belle Plain, Kansas, for shipment to the rat-invaded town of Hugo, Colorado.

The Atchison (Kansas) *Daily Champion*
Sunday, December 4, 1886, p3

Wagon, Ho!

The Bloom (Ford County) *Telegram* is responsible for
the statement that a wagon load of cats passed
through that town recently on their way west, where
they are in demand at $1.00 each.
    Arkansas City (Kansas) *Daily Traveler*
    Sunday, April 22, 1888, p4

Pussycat Profits

A man was in Dubuque, Iowa, recently buying cats,
for which he paid from 50 cents to $1 each, according
to age and size. He was shipping them to Dakota,
where he said they sold for $3 each.
    Weekly Chieftain, Vinita, Oklahoma
    Thursday, April 25, 1889, p1
    Red Cloud Chief, Red Cloud, Nebraska
    Friday, April 26, 1889, p2

More Trouble for Dawson
Steamer Rosalie Takes Cats
of Vocal Reputation North

Steamer *Rosalie* Capt. O'Brien sailed last evening from
Lynn canal ports. Among her passengers was H.J.
Coleman, an attorney from Wisconsin. He is taking
with him to Dawson a large crate of cats, whose vocal

organs furnished discordant music as the steamer left the dock. Mr. Coleman intends to dispose of the felines at Dawson for fancy prices as rat-exterminators. It is said that Purser W.P. Morrow charged each of the animals first-class fare.

A.L. Rhynd, another passenger is bound for Dawson. He has with him a big Klondike outfit.

The Seattle (Washington) *Star*
Thursday, July 13, 1899, p3

A Little of Everything

A Washington man has started for the Klondike with a large crate of cats on which he expects to make a fortune. In Dawson the rats are so troublesome that cats sell at from $20 to $50 each, irrespective of good looks, and he estimates that he will clean up $3,000 on his cat shipment. And that raises the question how did the rats get to Dawson? How do rats get anywhere? They are natural pioneers and always reach a new country a year or two ahead of their natural enemy, the cat. Neither Artic frost nor tropic fire deters the rat.

The Medford (Oregon) *Mail*
Friday, July 21, 1899, p1

Chapter Seven

Cat Prospecting

Once cats reached mining towns, they made news for their idiosyncrasies or their unusual accomplishments, not the least of which was survival, often under extraordinary circumstances. Mining communities were dangerous locales, often reducing the lifespans for both man and beast.

In early mining camps prospectors battled each other for mining claims and entertainment. If cats even made it to those primitive enclaves, they were subject to cruel pranks by entertainment-starved men, attacks by dogs or wild animals, accidents that claimed lives and limbs, and a precarious day-to-day existence on the edge of civilization.

As corporate industrial mining evolved to replace the lone prospector or a handful of partners with visions of wealth, the dangers boomed as well for both humans and animals. Mining towns were noisy enclaves with the continuous roar of stamping mills, the periodic rumble of underground explosions, the din of all-night dance halls and saloons, the clatter of freight and ore wagons, and the hullabaloo of hardened men seeking temporary refuge from their tedious and dangerous jobs. While everyone sought wealth, the riches in mining communities most often wound up in the soft palms of the managerial, legal and investor overseers rather than in the callused fingers of the mining laborers.

Cats wandered through these dangerous streets among men with unpredictable temperaments and hardened sensitivities. Women, the natural allies of cats, were often scarce or just as hardened as their male counterparts in mining communities.

Despite the dangers, cats survived and even thrived in these places, adapting to mining life in spite of the hardships. Due to the filth and debris that naturally accumulated in mining villages, rodents thrived, providing a plentiful and continuous source of food for feline appetites. With a plentiful supply of grub for their sustenance, cats then made frontier news according to their personalities or their odd circumstances. One cat actually collected gold, others survived arduous escapes from mineshafts, some greeted miners at the end of their daily shifts underground, and a few stood guard over warehouse goods against the constant threat of rats and mice.

Even after the booms ended in these rags-to-riches-to-dust communities, a mother lode of cat tales lived on in the surviving editions of boomtown newspapers.

Miners & Miners Column

An amusing mining story comes from the Mocking Bird mine in the Warm Springs district in Montana. L.J. Rowen, who owns and works the mine, also owns a pet cat. This cat climbs up and down the shaft, through drifts, crosscuts, stopes and levels, and lives down there most of the time, being fed by the miners from the contents of their dinner pails. A brilliant idea struck Rowen the other day. He washed the [cat's] hair as clean to the skin as it could be washed. Then he panned the dirty water to the highest percentage and the entire cat assayed $18.31 on an assayer's scales. It is doubtful if any mine in the Rocky Mountains can assay better than $18.31 to the cat.

   Arizona Republic, Phoenix, Arizona,
   Monday, July 18, 1898, p7

Puss Had Gold Dust in Her Fur

Gold dust to the amount of $18.31 was found in the fur of a Montana cat the other day. She had been in the habit of wandering up and down shafts, drifts, cross-cuts and levels in the Mocking Bird mine. Her owner, a miner named Mike Rowen, washed her and afterward "panned" the water. In the course of her wanderings she had accumulated nearly $20 worth of gold—*Chicago Evening News*

   Medford (Oregon) *Mail*
   Friday, September 9, 1898, p8

Rats in Silver Mines
They Inhabit Slopes and Levels of the Deepest Mines
Capers of the Rodents
Far Under Ground the Usually Timorous Creatures Become Friendly with Man—Danger Signals

When the silver mines of the Comstock were first discovered and white men flocked to the country, the only rats seen were the bushy-tailed little animals called "mountain rats." These are not true rats, yet they have a "rat look" about the head. They build houses, consisting of piles of sticks, bark and dry weeds, after the manner of the muskrat, but on high and dry ground and generally against the trunk of a spreading cedar or scrub pine tree. These so-called rats vanished as soon as the first settlers began to intrude upon their haunts, using them as targets in their pistol practice, applying matches to their houses and making themselves disagreeable neighbors in various other ways.

Soon the brown rat made its appearance. This is the rat which follows civilization in all parts of the world. Wherever ships go, it goes. The first rats were brought to the Comstock from California in freight wagons—principally, most likely, in the big "prairie schooners," stowed away among boxes and crates of goods. Their rapid increase after their first appearance on the Comstock was astonishing. From ten to fourteen young are produced at a birth, and there are several litters each year; besides, a rat is a grandfather before he is a year old. Then, adds the *Engineering and Mining Journal*, the rats that colonized the Comstock towns encountered no enemies. There were no cats in the country.

Soon stores, barns, warehouses, hotels—the whole town—were swarming with rats. Cats were then brought over from California, and the first lot sold for $20 to $25 a head. Soon every prairie schooner that crossed the mountains had slung to it a big cage filled with cats of all colors and kinds. The price went down to $10, then to $5 a head, and finally so many cats arrived that they could not be given away. For some time, however, crates and cages filled with cats—or what was left of them after fighting all the way over the mountains—continued to arrive, and, no sale being found for them, they were turned loose in the town. Soon the whole place swarmed with cats, and the cat nuisance was worse than the rat nuisance, and it was a thousand times more vociferous.

The rats soon discovered the mines and found therein a congenial home and a home free from the terrifying presence of members of the feline tribe. Never was a cat seen in any of the lower levels of the mines, though they sometimes prowl about the old surface of the tunnels.

The Anaconda (Montana) *Standard*
Friday, November 18, 1892, p6

And the Cat Came Back
Made Its Way Underground Through the Mines
A Distance of Two Miles

Great things have been accomplished in Butte, wonderful achievements have been recorded here; Butte has made and unmade men and women. The queer and the curious have stalked the streets arm in

arm. Miners have fallen hundreds of feet down
shafts, drills have pierced men's bodies and those
men live today to tell of the experiences. Last
holiday's edition of the *Standard* told of the Butte city
on top of the ground and of the Butte city under the
ground.

It remained for a pet cat to make the journey from
West Butte to Meaderville underground, a distance of
two miles. This feat has just been concluded, and the
cat lives to tell its tale.

Last fall little Annie McGinn lost her pet cat. It
was last seen in November in an abandoned shaft
house west of the big Poulin hoist. A streetcar
conductor stepped into the shanty and frightened the
cat, which jumped down the shaft one hundred feet
deep. The cat survived and opened up a howling
contest all by itself. Everyday some of the streetcar
men would go over to the shaft and listen. The cat
still howled, but nothing could be done for it. Little
Annie was heartbroken. Her brother secured a long
rope and lowered it into the shaft, hoping that the
kitten would "catch on" and be hoisted out of its sad
predicament, but the cat only howled louder. Annie
used to carry bits of meat and bread over to the hole
and throw them down for the cat to eat.

After a couple of weeks, the moaning in the shaft
ceased. Annie gave up her pet as lost forever. The
streetcar crew forgot all about the sad affair, and
Christmas at Annie's home was not as cheerful for
the owner of the lost kitten as it might have been had
kittie not been so venturesome.

Early in the winter the miners in the Green
Mountain, the Mountain Con and other shafts in the
vicinity imagined they heard sounds similar to that

made by a sick infant. Later the same noises were heard in the Anaconda, Mountain View, Gray Rock, Modoc, Mountain Chief, Rarus and the other workings on the Meaderville slope.

Yesterday afternoon while some children were playing near the dump of the Colusa mine, they were startled upon beholding a cat tumbling down the pile of rock with a carload of waste that had just been dumped. The kitten meowed piteously as it rolled over; just in time to escape a big chunk that came bounding past, just as the feline fell into an old powder can at the base of the dump. The children ran to the rescue and found a sorry looking specie of the cat family. Its hair was matted and soiled; its eyes red; and it was sore and lame. The only mark of identification was the little ribbon about its neck, to which was attached a very small brass bell. The ribbon was damp, but the bell tinkled as it used to when kittie played with Annie last fall in West Centerville. The wonderful feline underground explorer will be returned to its owner at once.

The Anaconda (Montana) *Standard*
Thursday, February 16, 1899, p8
A version of this story also appeared in
The Mexia (Texas) *Evening Ledger*
Saturday, September 9, 1899, p4

Corner on Cats.

The prevalence of rats in the city of Deadwood, and the scarcity of the feline tribe has caused the latter to be in much demand, especially among our warehouse men and merchants. It is reported that the agent of the N.W.S.&T. Co. not having the fear of man or God before his eyes, added a fine specimen of the tribe to his already large stock on hand. The aforesaid feline in this cat happened to belong to a lady well known in theatrical circles, who after searching for many days for her lost Thomas in vain, was informed this morning that it was in the possession of the aforesaid gentleman.

She immediately hied her to his office and demanded her pet, but the soft impeachment was denied, and she went mournfully away, thinking to herself the biblical quotation, "All men are liars."

The Black Hills Daily Times, Deadwood, South Dakota, Friday, January 25, 1878, p4

A Remarkable Cat

Among the permanent fixtures of the Congress mining camp, at Martinez, is a cat of unusual intelligence for a member of the feline tribe. It is a great favorite with the brawny-armed, good-natured miners at work there. It is of "Thomas" persuasion in sex, and in color so black that he casts a shadow on the darkest nights. He takes his turn on the night shift as regularly as the gong rings to call the men. He escorts the men up the trail to the mine in groups, going up with the first squad and then returning meets each succeeding one and accompanies it to the mine. When all are at work, he goes from one shift to another where the men are at work, and never leaves the mine until the shift is called off in the morning, unless there are visitors during the night.

In the latter case he is sure to hear them approach, and will come down the trail until he meets them, when he will escort them to the mine and show them the greatest courtesy by accompanying them through it. When they leave, however, he again joins the miners at work as before, going from one opening to another, apparently superintending the work.

When the night shift leaves, he follows the men to the boarding house, but rarely eats anything there, and never any cooked food, and then accompanies the day shift back to the mine. After all are at work, he lies down on a sack of ore or anything convenient for about an hour, when he disappears, and a search warrant would not discover his whereabouts until the gong sounds again for the men to go to work at night. He keeps up this habit as religiously as though the entire responsibility of the work rested on him, and no amount of persuasion can induce him to remain in the office or lodging rooms at night for any length of time when there is a force of men at work.

The cat belonged to Dennis May, who kept him for about two years, and who tells a remarkable story of his extreme sensitiveness. A little over a year ago, during the stormy weather of winter when navigation was practically impossible, Mr. May ran short of provisions and there was nothing in his cabin but bacon and beans, both of which the cat refused to eat. May angrily remarked that if he couldn't eat bacon and beans, he could leave camp. Getting out of the cabin shortly after, the cat disappeared, and nothing was seen of him for two months, when he returned again and has been a constant resident ever since.

Weekly Journal-Miner, Prescott, Arizona
Wednesday, February 22, 1888, p4

The Defunct Felines

It is only Dan De Quille who is capable of producing the following which appears in the *Virginia Enterprise* of Sunday: It is estimated that between fifteen and twenty thousand cats perished in the flames that lately licked half of our city from the side of Mount Davidson. The estimate is probably too high, as it appears to us that we miss no more than about ten or twelve thousand—that is, in a general way.

We, however, particularly miss and mourn no more than two or three hundred. These were favorites of our neighborhood that were wont nightly to do gambols and execute difficult musical selections for our diversion. How often, when the witching hour marking the noon of night was stealing in, have we seen some giant of the feline horde—a fighter from Bitter Creek—mount the giddy height of a neighboring firewall and sound his war-like bugle. We can see him now, as with arched back reared against the sky like some rounded chapparal hill, and erect tail waving like a cedar in a storm, he stands, in his sphere according to his knowledge, a defiant Ajax.

The moon is playing at hide and seek among a floating archipelago of clouds as he thus stands up and defines his position categorically as the boss fighter of the town. Another yell of warlike portent tells that the challenge is accepted and another Ajax appears upon the wall, arches his back and waves an angry tail. The pair draw their feet well beneath them, dig their claws into the wall and cautiously creep forward, ever and anon uttering sounds that would seem great though they came from the lungs of a pair of adult mastodons.

The friends and allies of the champions make their appearance on the roofs of surrounding houses and sheds, utter their several war cries and deploy as skirmishers. The two champions come together like rocks rolled from the sides of opposite hills; the skirmishers, with green eyes flashing, engage in all directions and the battle has become general. The air is rent with howls, shrieks, groans and gurgles—all the house tops are covered with hair. Half a dozen soda bottles and as many old boots crash down upon the roofs and against the walls; there is spit, a sputter and a fizz; then all is as silent as the tomb. Where now are those heroes and their heroic followers?

Alas, their calcined bones alone are left in the places where they once frisked and fought! All are gone! The tortoise-shell of the old maid, the mighty Maltese of the old bachelor, the pet cats that used to sleep on the counters and bite all who stroked them, and the wild cats that dropped down from places and stared at one in the night—all gone! The great fire cremated them all. In vain they darted from shed to stable and from stable to sidewalk with their tails erect and smoking or all aflame. Their time had come and they were either cooked in their holes or roasted as they ran. Let all true lovers of the cat join in and wail a villainous caterwaul!

Nevada State Journal, Reno, Nevada
Tuesday, December 28, 1875, p2

Defunct Felines Lauded

There's a silver lining to the Virginia City cloud, in the fact that from fifteen to twenty thousand prowling pussy cats are estimated to have gone up in the flames of the recent conflagration.

St. Louis Globe-Democrat
Thursday, January 13, 1876, p2
Dallas (Texas) *Daily Herald*
Saturday, January 15, 1876 p1

Women Scarce

An exchange has this: There is a mining camp called Bachelor's Rest about sixty miles north of Tucson, A.T., and the population now numbers upwards of 800. There is not a woman nor cat in the camp, and 200 men have advertised for wives in a Tucson paper. They must be of good character and understand the duties of a household. The richest miners offer a dowery of $40,000. You will notice that it says there is not a woman or cat in camp. We trust that our lady readers will not for a moment imagine that we use these words in a synonymous sense. Furthermore, we do not publish this in order to create an exodus of our marriageable ladies.

The Eugene (Oregon) *Guard*
Tuesday, January 8, 1895, p2

Comstock Rats and Cats
How They Combine to Raid on Property
Mysterious Cat Calls and Barkings
That Puzzle the Watchmen

During the past ten months no less than five regular raids have been made on the Fairfax hoisting works. The last of these was yesterday morning and the thieves got nothing, for the reason that nothing was left for them to get except the engines and foundation on which they stand. The watchman says it is impossible for any one man to guard against these thieves. He may stay on the grounds eighteen hours out of the twenty-four, but the moment he leaves for his meals, or for any other purpose vacates the works for half an hour, a raid is made.

In the five visits the thieves have made to the works, they have carried off twelve boxes of candles, one box of giant powder cartridges, $25 worth of fuse, a grindstone weighing about 200 pounds, a set of blacksmith's tools, and all the wood and lumber that was loose or could be broken off anywhere along the works. The watchman has done his best to prevent these thefts, but all without avail. He has left the works, pretending to come to town for his meals then has wheeled about and gone to the works without ever being able to catch any one in the act of removing property. All he has been able to detect was that he was followed and watched by one set while another was at work. He discovered this through hearing sounds as of cats calling to another at times when he turned back to go toward the works, or when he was coming toward them from his meals.

It is a well-known fact that it has been necessary to surround some of leading mining works in this city with high board fences in order to prevent the frequent raids on wood, lumber, tools, and other articles of value. No one watchman could guard the grounds. The thieves came in gangs of from six to ten, and by means of cat calls and other signals kept their partners constantly posted in regard to every step taken by the watchman. Thus, when he was on the north side of the works, the thieves were busy on the south side, and as he moved around toward the south active operations began on the north, signals being given by the barking of dogs and mewing of cats from persons secreted in lumber piles and other places whence the motions of the watchman could be observed as he went on his rounds.—*Virginia Enterprise*

Weekly Nevada State Journal, Reno, Nevada
Saturday, December 31, 1881, p1

Pacific Coast Items

Cat-poisoning is now lively in some parts of the town, says the Virginia (City) *Enterprise.* There is ample field for this industry along the whole Comstock range. Times have changed in this city since the days when a blear-eyed, lop-eared old tomcat was thought cheap at $20. Not a few old settlers will remember when cats were brought over the mountains by freight teams in coops such as are now used for the transportation of chickens. Of course, they fought all the way over the mountains, and when the remnants of a lot were taken out in this city it was thought good luck to get out a cat with even one eye.

The Record-Union, Sacramento, California,
Wednesday, June 16, 1880, p2

Altitude Sickness

One of the queerest of the many queer things about Leadville is that in all the length and breadth thereof there lives not a single cat. Cats have been imported here by the hundreds and in all varieties of color, breeding and size; but not one has ever survived the second week of residence. No one seems to understand why it is that the cats all die, but they do. The healthiest, sleekest cat in St. Louis, if brought to Leadville would lose all interest in life the moment it reached here, and after moping around in a sickly and disconsolate way for a few days would resignedly have a fit and give up the ghost.

A saloonkeeper on State Street brought a big strong Maltese from Denver a few days ago, hoping the animal would survive the fits long enough to become acclimated; but it was no use. The cat had a fit the first day, two or three the second, and then the number of attacks increased in a geometrical progression until, as the saloon-man said, "There were more fits than cat, and the cat had to give in."— *St. Louis Globe-Democrat*
Fort Worth (Texas) *Daily Gazette*
Saturday, August 30, 1884, p3

Thin Air

In Leadville, Colorado, the atmosphere is too thin for cats, or their common prey, rats and mice, to live. What a blessing some persons in other places would consider it if they could have that atmosphere for a while, when the cats are on their back sheds at night, making enough noise to raise an Egyptian mummy.
Colleyville (Kansas) *Weekly Journal*
Saturday, September 6, 1884, p3

No Cats

There is not a single cat within the limits of the town of Leadville, Colorado. Cats have been imported there by the hundreds, and in all varieties of color and size, but not one has ever survived the second week of residence. However, as there are no rats and mice in Leadville, there is no real need of cats, and it makes little difference whether they live or die. The thin atmosphere at that altitude (10,200) is as fatal to the vermin as to their foe, and the inhabitants are thus mercifully spared the inflictions of both.—*Chicago Inter-Ocean*

Wyandotte Gazette, Kansas City, Kansas
Friday, November 7, 1884, p1

That Lecture

Prof. Hoenschel's lecture at the M.E. church on Saturday night last was highly enjoyed by an appreciative audience. Pike's Peak was his subject and he interspersed anecdotes with solid facts in such a way as to hold the attention of his audience. … Cats can't live at Leadville, but the man who made the most money on his investment in '59—the first year of the Pike's Peak excitement—was the man who took out a load of cats. They cost him nothing, but sold for good round prices to the miners—to stand over their flour, which at $25 per sack, was too dear to be turned over to the army of wood-rats that preceded the gold seekers and the mice that went along for company. … The lecture was good, and as the cats were excluded, we can say without fear of contradiction that the talk was enjoyed by the entire audience.

The Alma (Kansas) *Signal*
Saturday, April 18, 1896, p1

A Deserted Mining Camp

J.M. Robinson writing from Meadow Lake, gives interesting facts regarding the once famous "mining camp." He states that the camp is all gone to the dogs and the mines about the place, with their machinery and hoisting works, are gradually molding into decay, and there is nothing but ruin everywhere. The town is now occupied by ten men, two women, two cats, a dog (dying) and a mule, who occasionally amuses himself by kicking down a row of buildings. He kicks down one building at the end and the rest fall as a matter of course. Hundreds of houses have been crushed flat by the snow. One man claims fourteen buildings and is trying to occupy them all. Another man has located forty-six ledges and is waiting for some capitalist to come along and buy him out. Occasionally, a ground hog wanders into the streets or a bear comes in to inspect the town, which relieves the monotony considerably, and such visitors are always welcome. To visit such a spot reminds one of Hood's weird poem, "The Haunted House."

Daily Gazette, Las Vegas, New Mexico
Thursday, August 14, 1879, p1

Chapter Eight

Curtain and Cat Calls

Long before Andrew Lloyd Webber's Cats became the fourth-longest-running Broadway show in history, felines traipsed across frontier stages, sometimes intentionally and sometimes not.

If they were not an annoyance on the frontier, cats were often a source of amusement, both informally in their day-to-day existence and formally in various entertainment options of the time. From formal readings on cats to stage productions involving felines, kitties often provided a distraction from the vagaries of frontier life.

A black cat in a San Francisco theater, for instance, was believed by some, at least, to be the reincarnation of a deceased actor. A dramatic reading of Mark Twain's "Jim Wolf and the Tom-Cats," printed earlier in this volume, was one of the selections performed in Brownville, Nebraska. An account of two boxing cats in New York City even made an appearance in a Texas newspaper. One innovative theater manager used cats to promote upcoming plays, a trick he first employed in St. Louis before taking the tactic to Broadway in New York.

Not only amusement but also lawsuits were spawned by theatrical felines across the frontier. And, in one unfortunate misunderstanding, cats were shipped to Sacramento as food for one showman's animal exhibition.

So, cats entertained pioneers both in the theater and in the street.

Cat Reading

Mr. Geo. Lyon, Jr., the elocutionist, whom the "Blakes" have engaged for an entertainment Sept. 10, 1880, will present a programme which cannot fail to delight his audience. Among his selections are the "Creeds of the Bells," "Rums Maniac," "Horatius at the Bridge," "The Doom of Claudius and Cynthia," "Hunting a Mouse," Mark Twain's "Jim Wolf and the Tom-Cats" etc., etc. The opera house ought to be filled.

Nebraska Advertiser, Brownville, Nebraska
Thursday, September 2, 1880, p3

A Talented Cat
Its Appreciation of Shakespeare
Jeweled by an Actress
A Supposed Case of Metempsychosis (cq)
in a San Francisco Theater

The Baldwin Theater possesses a very peculiar black cat, who has probably received more attentions from dramatic celebrities, male and female, than any member of the feline tribe in the country. Selim is the name of the highly cultivated mouser, the title having been bestowed on him by some discriminating actor, who was doubtless impressed by the rather Oriental tastes of the sable pet. Exactly how or when Selim became one of the properties of the theater no one can tell. All at once he sprang into notice and favor as a habitue of the greenroom and the stage and soon made himself as much a feature of the establishment as anything with four legs and a mercurial disposition can possibly be. When the Fanny Davenport combination occupied the theater recently, Selim attracted unusual attention in the greenroom as there were several confirmed spiritualists in the company, who hold the Pythagorean doctrine of the transmigration of souls.

John Thompson, who can impose spiritual activity into any inanimate object from a doughnut to a chunk of coal, and bring a fusillade of raps out of an ordinary piece of furniture, pronounced Selim at first sight a reanimated actor.

Property Master Marcus, who was listening to Thespian Thompson's diagnosis, suggested that possibly Selim was the shadow of some snide song-and-dance man.

"In sooth thou speakest well, good Marcus," quoth the Thespian, "but we shall soon test the temper of his former dramatic ability," and forthwith Mr. Thompson hurled at the defenseless cat a chunk of Shakespearian blank verse that would have staggered Joe McAuliffe if it hit him anywhere within the scope of his intellectuality. Instead of rolling over and dying instantly, the wonderful cat faced the poetic avalanche as calmly as a duck would an April shower, and when Mr. Thompson, at the end of his declamation, fell exhausted and perspiring over the prompter's table, Selim was as calm as Eve.

"My life upon it," exclaimed Mr. Thompson as soon as he could collect the remnants of his breath, "Selim was a legitimate actor."

Selim, who was listening gravely, was plainly seen by Mr. Bouvier to nod his head approvingly, and in the general discussion that followed in the greenroom the conclusions were reached that Selim was certainly the spirit of some eminent actor who once strode the Baldwin stage.

Morris Peyser thought that Selim's appreciation of tragedy indicated that he might be the ghost of the talented William E. Sheridan, but Master Mechanic Abrahams was ready to make affidavits that the weird feline was none other than Frank Evan Rae, the Beau Brummel of the melodramatic stage.

"Why, one day when Margaret Mather put a pink ribbon round her neck, I saw him go up to the mirror and tie it into an elaborate bow with his forepaws," said Mr. Abrahams.

Whatever the former status of Selim may have been, his future in cat life at least is assured, for his position in the theater is as well defined as that of Manager Hayman himself. Selim is the stock pet and any spare affection which the actresses have to bestow goes to him. Fanny Davenport during her recent engagement never tired of caressing Selim and the cat's gallantry toward her was tireless. He met the actress every evening at the stage entrance and greeted her with a cordial purr and after receiving the expected caress, trotted after her to the door of her dressing room where he left her with a respectful "meow." While the star was on the stage Selim stood on the first entrance watching her with evident interest and wagging his tail cheerfully whenever the auditorium echoed with appreciative applause.

The fourth act of "La Tosca," where Scarpia presses his unwelcome attentions on the heroine, affected Selim in an unusual manner, but his emotions have so far overcome his regard for stage etiquette as to lead him to dash from the wings on the stage and aid the actress in her struggles with the athletic Scarpia.

That Selim is a cat of the most extraordinary kind was shown by the conquest of Frank Willard, Miss Davenport's stage manager. When the Davenport combination occupied the theater, Assistant Treasurer Peyser called Willard's attention to the fact that Selim was regarded as something supernatural. Mr. Willard, who is quite a connoisseur in cats and a skeptic of the strongest type, smiled at the story, but before two days he was a firmer believer than anybody in the superstition about Selim. The phenomenal intelligence of the stage pet so impressed Mr. Willard that Selim got more privileges than were granted to the most favored bipeds of the company. The unheard of liberty of sitting on the prompt table during rehearsals was allowed Selim, and in the fourth act he was permitted to occupy the first entrance without drawing forth the vigorous reprimand that such a crime calls forth when a human biped is the offender.

Miss Davenport at the close of her recent engagement presented Selim with an expensive jeweled collar in presences of the full company.

The only person around the Baldwin Theater who discredits the superstition that Selim is the reincarnation of some actor's spirit is Forrest Seabury, who will have it that the wonderful cat is some departed scene-painter. Whenever Selim is not engaged downstairs, he wanders up to the paint frame and sits for hours at a time watching the pictorial work with an interest that is altogether unfeline.

Selim's almost insane antipathy to the attaches of snide dramatic sheets shows, however, that artist Seabury is wrong and that the wonderful cat is imbued with the soul of a true actor.

Selim knows every offensive scribbler [critic] by sight, and when he catches a glimpse of them behind the scenes, flies into an ungovernable rage. His form swells to gigantic proportions, his sleek back becomes corrugated and the bristles on his inflamed tail stand out like spikes on a telegraph pole. His eyes blaze with fury and his whole aspect denotes the progress of a regular whirlwind of passion. If the intruders ask for an interview with the star who may be playing, Selim's rage finds expression in whines and howls which Charley, the doorkeeper, interprets into such words as "blackmail," "scurrility," etc. It is evident that whatever branch of the dramatic art Selim followed in his former life, he learned to hate the newspaper scribes cordially, and when he displays his feelings toward them, most of them are inclined to beat a hasty retreat.

Though apparently well advanced in years Selim has all the true Thespian's admiration of the opposite sex, and his four-footed female admirers are numerous; whenever he wants to show his partiality toward some sleek dame of his tribe, he introduces her behind the scenes and during the Davenport engagement appeared to be so beset with applications for free passes that Doorkeeper Charley had to repress the crowd with a club. In every other respect but his blind infatuation for the other sex, Selim is a most exemplary cat, and though he can chew tobacco like a forty-niner and drink beer, he never carries these habits to excess. His gallantry, however, occasionally scandalizes the staid members of the company, but Manager Hayman overlooks all Selim's moral obliquities, believing that he is a mascot of the most pronounced type. Doorkeeper Charley has orders to keep Selim supplied with delicate cutlets of liver when the ordinary forage of the theater, such as rats, mice and cockroaches runs low. Another of the doorkeeper's duties is to groom Selim once a week, but the post of tonsorial manipulator of the cat's whiskers is a sinecure, as the ladies of the ballet are constantly titivating Selim and bestowing their affections on him in a way that would drive the bald-headed holders of front seats wild with envy.

The latest rumor round the Baldwin Theater about Selim is that Mr. Bouvier, who is quite a playwright, is constructing a drama with Selim as one of the leading characters. Selim is the pet of the heroine, who is restrained by hard-hearted parents from visiting her unfortunate lover, who is incarcerated in the fourth story of a Bush-street boarding house for non-payment of dues. Selim, to please his fond mistress, defies a ferocious bull-terrier in the back yard of the hashery, and scaling to the bedroom of the imprisoned lover with a clothes line wound round his tail, sets the captive free. In the last scene the happily wedded pair are shown by the domestic hearth surrounded by thirteen beautiful children, while Selim grown old and gray, but still as joyous and talented as ever, sits on the windowsill and sings "Auld Lang Syne."

It is thought that this will cap the climax in the way of pure and emotional domestic dramas.

San Francisco Chronicle
Sunday, October 13, 1889, p8

Oakland's Cats

Oakland is renowned as the great cat city in America. Cats may be seen at almost any time of day, and heard at any time of night. If Oakland honestly enjoys a reputation for one thing, it does it in the cat business. An incident in this connection may be apropos: A showman who was exhibiting an anaconda in Sacramento, and giving it daily a rabbit for food, having occasion to print some "poster" bills, telegraphed his agent in San Francisco to "send 200 cuts immediately." The agent read it cats, and thinking the manager proposed to change the diet of the snake, sent out an army of men catching cats, and by night was able to ship nearly a hundred. The agent, in apologizing for not sending the whole two hundred, said he hoped the snake would have enough to "stay his stomach" until he could go over to Oakland, as Oakland was full of cats, and he thought he could fill the order at one haul.

Oakland (California) *Tribune*
Friday, June 12, 1874, p1

Two Thousand Cats
Turned Loose on the Streets of New York
Homeless and Friendless

Two thousand cats were turned out of Niblo's theater this morning, says a recent New York special, to find their respective ways home or take their luck with strangers. Each cat was conspicuously labeled, but as the labels were alike, they probably proved of no assistance to the unfortunate animals. The affair was the outcome of five-line advertisement in a newspaper, and it certainly tends to demonstrate the value of advertising.

The advertisement announced that 5,000 cats were wanted at Niblo's stage door (at) 10 o'clock on Friday morning. Nobody at the theater knows the hour at which the first cat arrived, but long before the appointed time Crosby Street was crowded with various kinds of people. Every one of them had at least one cat. They were carried in arms, in baskets and in overcoat pockets. One enterprising boy brought eight, all huddled together in a mail bag. There were some feline protests delivered in short, plaintive yamps, but as a rule cats were too much astonished at the circumstance to say anything about it.

About 9:30 Mr. Ben Stern, whose fertile brain had evolved the scheme, appeared at the stage door. He decided not to wait till 10 o'clock, and with the employees of the theater began to take in the cats. The candidates endured no civil-service examination. They were all equal in Stern's eye, regardless of size, color or disposition. One requisite only was enforced—the cats had to be alive. As they were delivered up various bargains were struck with the owners. Most of them were satisfied with tickets of admission to the *Gallery God*, beginning next week, one ticket for each cat. Others, either from conscientious scruples against the stage or from financial difficulties, preferred to take cash, and these were rewarded with dimes.

One youngster with a glum face handed in three kittens, saying: "Ma says you can have these an' welcome. We've got more'n we want and we're going to keep a tom."

Stern refused to profit by the mother's generosity and gave the boy a ticket and a dime.

The crowd hung about after all the cats were in, waiting to see what would happen. Some of them had anxiously stipulated no harm should be done to puss, and the theater people had accordingly told them the scheme. It occurred to Stern that if the cats were turned loose in that crowd every one would be caught, stripped of its tag and returned for a new bargain. So, the employees drove the crowd away.

Meantime, every cat had been taken in hand gently and supplied with a big tag, fastened about the neck with a string. On each side of the tag was an announcement of the Christmas pantomime to be produced at Niblo's theater. When the streets were well clear of possible speculators in cats, the animals were freed. They were glad enough to get out of the theater, and most of them set off at a lively scramble. Few went any further in the first spurt than across the street. Then they paused in various attitudes, some looking nervously about with one free paw in the air, others eyeing the walls, with a view to jumping over, and some sat calmly down and thought about it. The theater people assisted the cats in getting a move on, and in a few minutes all of 2,000 or more had disappeared.

Mr. Stern tried this scheme in St. Louis three years ago, and to test the efficacy of the advertisement he assigned a man to follow one cat and see what became of her. She led him [on] a weary chase three times about nearly the whole city, and at last, after ten hours, brought up at her home with the tag still on. It had been seen and read by a great many people in the course of the journey.

The Galveston (Texas) *Daily News*
Tuesday, December 10, 1889, p11

Now You See Them, Now You Don't

Hermann, the magician, has sued a manager at Sioux City to recover $5,000 damages for a pair of trick doves that were important confederates of the wizard. The manager's cat ate the magician's doves, and Hermann, with all his skill in magic, could not bring them to life again. Hence the suit.

The Record-Union, Sacramento, California
Saturday, April 1, 1893, p7

Music and Drama

In "A Trip to Chinatown" a cat is used in the first act. A cat is rather a difficult thing to handle as theatrical property, and is usually kept under lock and key. One night last week as Welland Strong stood in the wings ready to go on, it was discovered that the cat had escaped; it couldn't be found anywhere. Harry Conner, who plays Welland Strong so cleverly, was frantic. Nothing could be done. He would have to go on without the cat. Conner received his cue and rushed forward when Miss Pussy jumped into his arms, where she quietly nestled and kept on purring during the entire scene. The cat knew her business, and has been added to the regular staff of Hoyt and Thomas. She has now the run of Hoyt's Madison Square Theater with unlimited quarts of fresh milk, which stage manager R.A. Roberts has especially ordered, and which he himself feeds her with.

The Record-Union, Sacramento, California
Saturday, December 19, 1891, p6

Stage Fright

Mme. Modjeska is superstitious about cats. She has never given a performance in her life without having a cat on the stage hidden away somewhere. In large cities her property plot always calls for a cat at every performance, and before the curtain is rung up she assures herself that the animal is there. When she is playing one- and two-night stands, she carries a cat with her. She firmly believes that she owes all her success in life to her adherence to this rule.

Morning Oregonian, Portland, Oregon
Thursday, September 9, 1886, p6

Hand Shadow Art

A true art is claimed as a development of the familiar diversion of making rude figures by the shadow of the hands on the wall. Trewey, a French artist, has added great variety to these shadow pictures, and his fast-increasing list already numbers more than 300 new forms. By patient exercise he has given his hands great suppleness, enabling him not only to represent the most diverse figures upon a screen, but to give them motion and life. The swan smoothing his plumage, the bird taking flight, the cat making its toilet, the tightrope dancer, who, after saluting the public, rubs chalk on her feet before walking on the rope, are among the silhouettes produced of such wonderful accuracy that one can scarcely believe they are shadows of the hands alone.

The Record-Union, Sacramento, California
Saturday, May 19, 1888, p3

Cats With Gloves
Unusual Method of Entertainment in New York
Two Feline Boxers Daily Contest for Pugilistic Honors

A most exciting exhibition of pugilism takes place twice daily in a theater in New York. Women and Children, as well as men, witness it. They applaud wildly at the movements when the combatants are most energetically seeking to render one another unconscious. The fighters are Jim Corbett and Peter Jackson. These are not their right names, but have been conferred by Professor J.W. Hampton, who has charge of the sparring exhibition which they give at Keith's Union Square Theater.

It must further be explained that the pugilists are not men, but cats. Their contest is not on that account any less fierce, serious and exhilarating. On the contrary, it is rather more so. The cat's natural method of fighting, as most people are probably aware, is to bite with his teeth and to scratch with all four feet. He uses his hind legs with great energy when he gets his opponent down. This natural method is very effective, and would, no doubt, make a public exhibition very interesting, but such an entertainment would hardly be allowed. The cats have, therefore, been instructed in the rules of boxing as laid down by the Marquis of Queensbury.

Corbett and Jackson are both heavily built tomcats of strongly pugnacious instincts, confirmed and developed by several years of hard fighting without gloves. From the time that they reached adolescence, it is probable that neither of them ever passed an evening without engaging in fierce and bloody strife. They have received wounds on many a well-fought roof before they emerged from private life to give public exhibitions.

Like the namesake of one of them, both are given to a somewhat excessive use of language. But in extenuation it should be said that their language is principally bad, consisting of swearing and yowls. They do not indulge in rhetoric nor dialects. Neither of them pretends to be a gentleman, and anything else but a common fighting cat.

Corbett is white and Jackson is black-and-white. They cost their trainers 25 cents apiece, and were brought in by a boy from somewhere. At least it is certain they were not pampered, fashionable cats, who had lost courage and sinew in a life of enervating luxury.

The writer witnessed a fight between Corbett and Jackson the other night, says the *New York Journal*. Before the event each sat on a stool waiting for the fray. When time was called their trainer picked them up and placed them in a ring, consisting of a square board, having ropes and wooden stakes around it and placed on a high basket.

Each wore heavy gloves. They stood upright most of the time, but did not exhibit much science. They proved, however, that they were game to the last drop of their blood. The trainer had repeatedly to interfere in order to prevent the fight from degenerating into a rough and tumble chewing and scratching contest. Corbett several times fouled his opponent by biting and by attempting to scratch with his hind feet. In spite of their outrageous conduct Professor Hampton allowed the fight to proceed. It was the intention that it should be carried on to a knockout, and so it was. The fight lasted four rounds and ended with the knocking out of Peter Jackson. To that result, however, Professor Hampton largely contributed by helping Corbett to throw his opponent over the ropes.

The Bryan (Texas) *Daily Eagle*
Wednesday, June 17, 1896, p2

A Musical Cat

The *New York Sun* says that a young man who went the other evening to the home of A.N. White, the keeper of the morgue, heard the scale being run on the piano in the back parlor. "Who's practicing so industriously, Major?" the visitor asked. "Oh, that's Minnie," keeper White replied. "She's very fond of music. I'll introduce you to her. Here Minnie, Minnie, Minnie." The instant he called the name a handsome black-and-white cat bounded into the room. "She's the piano player," keeper White said. "When she sees the piano open, she jumps on the keys and runs up and down the board until somebody comes and plays for her. Then she sits down and listens and purrs."

The Record-Union, Sacramento, California
Saturday, February 4, 1888, p8

ACKNOWLEDGEMENTS

My research into cats in the Old West was spawned by a comment by Jefferson Glass and a writing assignment by Mike Cox. They along with Beverly Waak are due thanks for starting me on this fascinating historical journey.

I was delighted when *New York Times* bestselling author Chris Enss offered to do the foreword for this volume. She is a wonderful writer and a great friend to my wife and me.

Archivists who have been especially helpful over the years are Dr. Tai Kreidler of the Southwest Collection at Texas Tech University and Suzanne Campbell and Shannon Sturm of the West Texas Collection at Angelo State University. I am also indebted to Shannon for locating the photo for the cover of *More Cat Tales of the Old West*. As you might imagine, cat photos from the frontier period are hard to find.

Thanks also are due to San Angelo photographer Jim Bean, who colorized the ASU photo for publication and designed the book cover.

Finally, I must thank Harriet Kocher Lewis, editorial director for Bariso Press, for her fine editing and proofing support. Every writer needs a good editor, and she is the best. I have been blessed throughout my writing career to have her at my side as my wife.

ABOUT THE AUTHOR

Preston Lewis is the award-winning author of more than 40 western, historical and juvenile novels. In 2021 he was inducted into the Texas Institute of Letters for his literary accomplishments.

Western Writers of America (WWA) has honored Lewis with two Spur Awards, one for best article and the second for best western novel. He has received two Will Rogers Gold Medallion Awards for written western humor and two more for western short stories.

Lewis is a past president of WWA and the West Texas Historical Association, which has named him a fellow. He holds a bachelor's degree from Baylor University and a master's degree from Ohio State University, both in journalism. Additionally, he has a second master's degree in history from Angelo State University.

He lives in San Angelo, Texas, with wife Harriet.

E-mail: prestonlewisauthor@gmail.com
Facebook: prestonlewisauthor
Website: prestonlewisauthor.com